Girls

are

from

Saturn

Boys are from Jupiter

Kathryn Lamb

Kathryn Lamb lives 'quietly' in Gillingham, Dorset, with her husband, Adrian Bovey, and their six children and two hamsters. Adrian has three teenage children.

Without the help of all these people (not so much the hamsters) she would have found it a lot more difficult to write this book. She would like to thank them all, including some very special grandparents.

Kathryn draws cartoons for Private Eye and The Oldie. She has illustrated a number of books for Piccadilly Press including: *For Weddings, A Funeral and When You Can't Flush The Loo; You're My Best Friend – I Hate You; A Right Royal History; The Good, The Bad and The Ghastly: World War II* and *The Good, The Bad and The Ghastly: The Wild West*.

She is also the author of the extremely well-reviewed *Help!* series. *Help! My Family is Driving me Crazy!* was selected by The Bookseller as one of a hundred best books for Spring 1997: '. . . *it hits just the right humorous note.*'

Other books by Kathryn Lamb,
published by Piccadilly Press:
HELP! MY FAMILY IS DRIVING ME CRAZY!
HELP! MY SOCIAL LIFE IS A MESS!
HELP! LET ME OUT OF HERE!
BOYWATCHING!

Girls
are
from
Saturn

WHEN WORLDS COLLIDE

Boys are from Jupiter

Kathryn Lamb

Piccadilly Press · London

for my children

Text and illustrations copyright © 1998, Kathryn Lamb

3 5 7 9 10 8 6 4 2

All rights reserved. No part of this publication may be
reproduced, stored in a retrieval system, or transmitted
in any form or by any means electronic, mechanical,
photocopying, recording or otherwise, without
the prior permission of the copyright owner.

The right of Kathryn Lamb to be identified as Author
and Illustrator of this work has been asserted by her in
accordance with the Copyright, Designs and
Patents Act 1988.

Printed and bound by Bookmarque Ltd.
for the publishers Piccadilly Press Ltd,
5 Castle Road, London NW1 8PR

A catalogue record for this book is available
from the British Library

ISBNs 1 85340 581 7 (trade paperback)
1 85340 576 0 (hardback)

Design by Judith Robertson
Cover design by Louise Millar

Contents

Intergalactic Glossary of Astral Abbreviations and Other Interplanetary Info

Saturn Girl

Jupiter Boy

F.A.B. Favourite Alien Being (this gorgeous, mouth-watering apparition is otherwise known as the Heavenly Body from Jupiter or the Super-Sexy Thang from Saturn)

P.E.F. Potential Embarrassment Factor (you are particularly aware of this when your parents and your F.A.B. are in the same room together

E.T.s Embarrassing Things (another name for parents. Alternatively, the sort of things that parents are inclined to say from time to time, particularly when your F.A.B. is present)

Saturnspeak Girl Talk

Jupiterjargon Boy talk

Clingfilm Syndrome Total inability to leave your F.A.B. alone. You are totally wrapped in him or her (so to speak)

Plutonian Pothole Bad thing to fall down – a problem

Cosmic Crowd Friends

Star Attraction What happens when Jupiter and Saturn like each other

Cosmic Fallout What happens when they don't

Heavenly Body Spray Available at all good interplanetary perfume shops

Introduction

Once upon a time there was a beautiful planet with rings around it, populated only by girls. BORING??!? No, it wasn't. The girls on Saturn had never heard of boys, so they lived together in peace and harmony since they never argued over boyfriends or felt the need to compete for the attentions of the same boy. They sorted out any other problems they had by talking them through, listening to others and sharing in group discussions, sometimes

THE GIRLS FROM SATURN

giving each other shoulder massages along with helpful advice. They did feel occasionally that something was missing, but they weren't quite sure what. It seemed that they were running out of things to give each other helpful advice about.

Then came the BOYS. They landed on Saturn in an enormous spaceship that gleamed and shone jet black with a white lightning stripe along its side (the boys spent most of their spare time lovingly polishing their

THE BOYS
FROM JUPITER

8

beloved spaceship, and occasionally taking it to pieces and putting it back together again to make it go faster).

As the doors opened, a shaft of blinding white light temporarily dazzled all the girls. When their eyes grew accustomed to the light, they were equally dazzled by the sight of the boys themselves. The boys stood staring open-mouthed, similarly transfixed by the sight of the girls and, just for a moment, they forgot all about their beloved spaceship.

The girls started shouting out things they had never been heard to say before, such as:

'Wow! They're GORGEOUS!'
and:
'I like the one with the black wavy hair!'
and:
'That one's MINE!'

This last comment signalled the end of the girls' peaceful and harmonious existence. For it was the start of the

GREAT FALLING OUT

The Great Falling Out (which wasn't so great) meant that the girls all started arguing over which of the boys was THEIRS, and whether one of the boys had looked at them ('No, he looked at ME!'), and which one was the most fanciable, and so on. Then they argued over who was most likely to attract the boys and began to compete with each other with clothes/make-up, etc.

The boys watched all this with increasingly baffled expressions on their faces and reacted to the girls in various different ways:

• Some acted cool and casual, and feigned indifference.

• Others spent hours in front of the mirror preparing themselves to meet the strange beings from Saturn.

• Some became silent and moody, and worried the Parents from Jupiter.

• Others shut themselves away in their rooms and listened to music.

• A few simply shook their heads in a puzzled manner and turned their attentions back to polishing their beloved spaceship.

At this, an anguished cry went up from the assembled girls:

'OH MY GOD, THEY'RE NOT INTERESTED IN US!'
And they began making comments like:

'Is it the way I did my hair? Does it look stupid?'

and:

'Does my bum look enormous in these trousers?'

SO WHY DID THE GIRLS AND THE BOYS FEEL SO INSECURE?

This was because there was no communication between these two different beings – JUPITER and SATURN – and therefore there was no understanding. They felt drawn to each other (why else had the spaceship landed?), but they weren't quite sure how to deal with the DIFFER-ENCES between them.

Fact: The minds of boys and girls are DIFFERENT. It is very difficult to appreciate how different they are, as you cannot SEE them (try imagining that a boy's mind is square whereas a girl's is round).

This book will try to probe the mysterious corners of the male and female minds and explain some of their workings. It will also suggest strategies for creating inter-planetary harmony between the BOYS from Jupiter and the GIRLS from Saturn.

JUPITER
(THE BOYS FROM JUPITER WILL OFTEN BE REFERRED TO AS 'JUPITER' THROUGHOUT THIS BOOK)

SATURN
(THE GIRLS FROM SATURN WILL FREQUENTLY BE REFERRED TO AS 'SATURN' THROUGHOUT THIS BOOK)

BOY FROM JUPITER
('JUPITER')

GIRL FROM SATURN
('SATURN')

CHAPTER 1

Spotlight on Saturn and Jupiter

Please note: Any Boy from Jupiter may be referred to as just 'Jupiter'. Any Girl from Saturn may be referred to simply as 'Saturn'.

FAVOURITE ALIEN BEING
(F.A.B.)

So where did Saturn's Favourite Alien Being (F.A.B.) – not to mention all his mates – come from? In what far-flung garage of the galaxy did they gather to admire the particularly shiny and new spaceship which Josh from Jupiter's mum gave him for his birthday?

In order to shed light on some of the peculiarities of life on Jupiter and Saturn, a small space probe was sent on a fact-finding mission. It was launched first into the letter-box of Josh from Jupiter's homeworld (and was nearly swallowed whole by the Dog from Jupiter).

A SMALL SPACE PROBE WAS LAUNCHED...

Jupiter At Home

• First, we enter Jupiter's Kitchenzone, where Josh is preparing a packed lunch, prior to setting off on a long cosmic cycle-ride with his mates from Jupiter.

Dad from Jupiter: 'Why don't you just take the whole fridge and be done with it? You're eating us out of house and homeworld!'

Mum from Jupiter: 'Oh come on, Jeremiah, dear! Josh is a growing boy! He needs to eat.'

Fact: Josh from Jupiter's mother (and any other mum from Jupiter) usually leaps to his defence. She looks after him, and occasionally fusses over him which causes him some embarrassment, especially if she does this in front of his mates, or in front of the Girlfriend from Saturn. For Jupiter, the Potential Embarrassment Factor (P.E.F.) of having parents is extremely high (more of this later . . .).

• Next, we enter Jupiter's Living-roomzone, where Josh is sprawled all over the sofa (boys are expert sprawlers – no other living creature manages to take up quite so much physical space, not even the Dog from Jupiter).

JUPITER IS AN EXPERT AT SPRAWLING

Josh is watching a football match on TV. His mother enters the room.

Mum from Jupiter: 'Josh, I've got some news for you. I'm expecting a baby!' Josh (averting his eyes with some difficulty from the television screen): 'Er . . . that's, er, amazing, Mum . . . I mean . . . er, I don't know what to say.' Suddenly he leaps into the air with a great cry of: 'Yes! YESSS!!! They've scored! Mum! Mum! Jupiter United have scored a goal! Do you realise what this means? Do you REALISE? They QUALIFY! Yes! They GO THROUGH!' He gives his mother a hug. Looking slightly dazed, she leaves the room.

Fact: Jupiter sometimes finds it difficult to deal with emotional matters or things that are too close to home. He

BOYS NEED ACTION

may focus on something such as a sport, which distracts him from more disturbing thoughts or feelings. He needs SPACE and ACTION.

• Next, we enter the Bedroomzone, which is Jupiter's OWN SPACE. Here he can relax, throw his possessions (or 'stuff') all over the place, think his own thoughts, dream his own dreams, and play his own music – until the Mum from Jupiter tells him to turn it down and to tidy his room. In some respects, life on Jupiter is not dissimilar to life on Saturn. The walls of Jupiter's Bedroomzone are likely to look different, however. They may be covered with posters relating to his favourite sport, or there may be a huge picture of the latest and most advanced kind of spaceship. There may even be one or two pictures of girls, but Jupiter may prefer the rest of his family (who *insist* on coming into his room from time to time) not to see too many of these (Potential Embarrassment Factor again). Jupiter is often an avid collector of Things. There may be a collection of fossils, interesting stones, model spaceships, or twenty-seven different kinds of cactus. A Visitor from Saturn may be invited to admire his collection of miniature hand-painted battle figures, or very rare Mercurial Moon Mice, or something similar.

Fact: Admiring any aspect of Jupiter's homeworld is a good way of paying him a compliment without embarrassing him.

It is just as well to be aware that Jupiter behaves differently in his own homeworld from the way he behaves when he is visiting the Saturn homeworld.

How Jupiter Behaves When He is at Home

• 'It's not my turn to do the washing-up. Look, I'm really tired. YOU do it. Mum, MUM. I'm tired! I had a hard day at school. No, I don't want to go to bed. My favourite programme's just about to come on.'

• TO HIS LITTLE SISTER: 'No, I'm not going to read to you. Can't you see I'm busy? GO AWAY!'

• TO THE DOG: 'Get out of the way of the television, you stupid animal! I can't see a thing. No, I'm NOT taking you for a walk. Forget it, you old fleabag!'

Please note: Jupiter Is Usually Polite When He Is Visiting Saturn Or A Friend's House.

• 'May I help you with the washing-up, Mrs Saturn? No, no, it's no trouble at all. Thank you for the delicious meal!'

- 'Is that your little sister? I've got a little sister. She's great. She likes me to read to her.'
- 'I like your dog. I've got a dog. He's wonderful, and great company. I love taking him for walks. Shall we take your dog for a walk?'

When he is in his own homeworld, Jupiter tends to relax. He doesn't mind too much what his mother, his little sister or the dog think of him. He is nice to them most of the time, but he doesn't feel the need to be at his best the whole time. He knows that they will accept his occasional changes of mood and still love him. ('It's his *age*, Jeremiah. He can't help it. It's all part of growing up. It's no use losing your temper with him. He will grow out of it, eventually. You just have to be patient . . .')

When he is visiting the Saturn homeworld, he is much more concerned about what other people think of him.

He cares what Saturn thinks of him. He is likely to be on his best behaviour. This is something of a strain for him, so Saturn should not be too disconcerted when he reverts to his normal behaviour (sprawling everywhere and refusing to do the washing-up) the moment he sets foot back on Jupiter.

Saturn At Home

(The small space probe – slightly battered after Josh whacked it out of the Bedroomzone window with his tennis racket – now directs its beam on to the Saturn homeworld.)

• First, we try to enter the Bathroomzone. It may not be possible to enter the Bathroomzone, because the door is locked, and Saturn will be in there for the next three hours, soaking in the bath, washing and dyeing her hair, and so on. Jupiter does not spend quite so much time in the Bathroomzone (although he has been known to bleach his hair), but prefers to sit in front of the TV or computer. Saturn, on the other hand, is drawn to the bathroom mirror as if by a strong magnet, and spends many hours in front of it, trying to improve her looks to the point where any boy from Jupiter will find her totally irresistible.

• Next, we enter Saturn's Bedroomzone, where you are left in NO DOUBT about her main area of interest – BOYS. She is obviously fascinated by life on Jupiter, because there are pictures and posters of handsome hunks in all directions. The floor and bed are littered with magazines from which she is in the process of cutting out more and more images of Jupiter. (Her magazines are all about Jupiter, whereas Jupiter's magazines are mostly about spaceships.) Of course, Saturn has plenty of other interests as well, but these temporarily go out of her mind when a Handsome Hunk or Heavenly Body from Jupiter floats into her field of vision.

• Saturn In Front Of The Televisionzone. Saturn is a keen follower of soaps and other 'people' dramas on television, since they deal with relationships (not spaceships) and feelings. Jupiter says that soaps are rubbish, and hides behind his spaceship magazine (although it is quite possible he is listening to every word). He prefers films with plenty of action, and sports programmes.

Fact: Saturn is usually more open with the rest of her family about her hopes, fears, dreams, worries, etc. than Jupiter is with *his* family (the P.E.F. levels on Saturn are lower).

• Girls Just Like To Have A Good Conversation (Importance Of The Phonezone On Saturn).

Sophie from Saturn: 'Dad – can I phone up Sarah? I really need to talk to her!'
Dad from Saturn: 'But you've just *seen* Sarah all day at school! You'll see her again tomorrow. Why on earth do you need to phone her NOW?'

To overcome the problem of having to break off a good conversation in order to go home and sleep, girls may arrange a sleepover party (the Saturn Sleepover) so that they can carry on the conversation all night.

GIRLS' SLEEPOVER PARTY

BOYS' SLEEPOVER PARTY

When Saturn Talks To Saturn

Saturn shares her thoughts and feelings with other girls. They listen to each other and offer advice as a sign of friendship. Needing help is not seen as a sign of weakness (as it often is on Jupiter). Girls relate to each other's experiences by admitting that they, too, have made mistakes, which shows that they are HUMAN. They start confessing to stupid things that they may have said or done, and at this point they may start giggling uncontrollably. This is extremely therapeutic. It is also the sort of behaviour that drives Jupiter round the bend.

The Saturn-to-Saturn Heart-to-Heart

Sarah from Saturn: 'How's it going, Susie?'

Susie from Saturn: 'Not well.'

Sarah: 'Want to talk about it?'

Susie: 'Yes.' (At this point Susie may even break down in tears at the sheer relief of having found a friend to talk to. She may rest her head on Sarah's shoulder briefly, and have a hug before she starts talking.)

Susie: 'You know what he said?'

Sarah: 'No. Tell me.'

Susie: 'He said he thought my doggie was goofy.'

Sarah: 'The insensitive brute! What did you say?'

Susie: 'I told him he was an insensitive brute, and that I love my dog very much, and I KNOW he isn't perfect, but that's got nothing to do with it, and he shouldn't say things like that because he must realise how it makes me feel.'

Sarah: 'What did he say?'

Susie: 'Nothing. He went on kicking his stupid football against the wall.'

Sarah: 'So what did you do?'

Susie: 'I told him he ought to say "Sorry".'

Sarah: 'What did he say then?'

Susie: 'He said, "Sorry".'

Sarah: 'Were you happy with that?'

Susie: 'No. I told him, "Sorry isn't good enough." '

Sarah: 'What happened next?'

Susie: 'He shouted, "See you!", and ran off. And, oh Sarah, the problem is I still like him. Loads! But I can't just forgive him for insulting my dog. And now he probably hates me too. And it's all so complicated.' (She bursts into tears again, and Sarah puts a comforting arm around her.)

FOR HOW LONG HAVE YOU SUFFERED FROM THESE STARS IN YOUR EYES?

Sarah: 'I know how you feel. I've been there.' (Saturn is always reassured to know that her friend has Been There, and has obviously got through it and survived.)

Sarah: 'I know he still likes you.' (Mutual morale-boosting is an important part of a Saturn-to-Saturn heart-to-heart.) 'Maybe you both need time on your own to unwind. You need a break. Then you can get your act back together. Why don't you come shopping with me?'

When Jupiter Talks To Jupiter

If Jupiter is upset about something, he tends not to discuss it. Instead, he throws himself into a sport or a difficult project (such as taking the whole spaceship to pieces and putting it back together again). If he can achieve something, he will feel better about himself, and there-fore more able to deal with the problem, whatever it is. He prefers to sort things out on his own, if he can.

Typical Talk When Jupiter Meets Jupiter (Mate-to-Mate Rather Than Heart-to-Heart)

PHASE ONE OF THE CONVERSATION: Exchange of Greetings.

James from Jupiter: 'Hello, Joe. How's things?'

Joe: 'Great. How about you?'

James: 'Fine. How's Susie?'

Joe: 'She's fine.'

James: 'Good on you. Lucky devil!'

OPTIONAL PHASE TWO OF THE CONVERSATION:
Sustained Bout Of Loud, Hearty Laughter Followed by
Interchange of Back-Slapping, Friendly Shoving or Mock
Fighting, Ribald Comments, Rude Jokes and Even Ruder
Noises – all of which is known as Friendly Banter.

PHASE THREE OF THE CONVERSATION: Enough of
This. Time for Action.

Joe: 'Fancy a game of football?'

James: 'Yeah, sure. Race you to the field!' (Friendly challenge.)

PHASE FOUR: There isn't one.

Note: Boys *do* discuss important matters with each other
from time to time, and, of course, they *do* have feelings.
It is just that their feelings tend to lie buried under self-
protective layers of words, whereas girls express their
feelings *through* words. Because of this tendency to hide
and conceal their true feelings, boys may have a tougher
time dealing with their emotions, since they are attempt-
ing to do so ON THEIR OWN (almost like an internal
test of strength and endurance), and Saturn should try to
understand this, and be patient.

THE SNAIL FROM JUPITER

Interplanetary Advice For Saturn

Don't put pressure on him to talk if he doesn't want to by repeatedly asking: 'What's wrong? Tell me!' This is like trying to prise an unwilling snail out of its shell. You will succeed only in injuring it (or injuring its pride, if it is a Snail from Jupiter).

Give him plenty of space and he will come out of his shell when he feels ready. If Jupiter comes to Saturn and wants to talk, that is fine.

Interplanetary Advice For Jupiter

Don't feel too pressurised when Saturn starts asking you hundreds of unfathomable questions, or seems to be expecting something from you. (What? You've no idea.) You could try:
• Asking the advice of your mum or any member of Saturn society you trust. They may be able to explain.
• Telling Saturn you have no idea what is going on, and asking her to explain.
• If you do feel the need to run away, you could try to soften the blow by suggesting you get together at another time, or just by being very friendly before saying goodbye.

When Saturn Talks To Jupiter
And Jupiter Talks To Saturn

This is when the problems (and the fun) begin. Saturn and Jupiter make the fundamental mistake of assuming that they are talking the same language, when in fact they are speaking two quite different languages:

SATURNSPEAK and JUPITERJARGON

This results in Interplanetary Communication Problems.

Although Saturn and Jupiter use the same words, they may use them in different ways, with different meanings, and that is when misunderstanding creeps in.

Basic Principles of Saturnspeak

Girls talk to REVEAL. They use words to help them UNDERSTAND and to feel CLOSE to each other. LISTENING is important and so is being HEARD.

Basic Principles of Jupiterjargon

Boys talk to CONCEAL. They prefer NOT to discuss relationships and their deepest feelings. They use words to distance themselves from subjects that are too personal or too complicated, and to convey to the rest of the world (which usually includes the Mates from Jupiter and, more particularly, Anyone from Saturn) that they are OK. Their best defence is not words but SILENCE, and it is VERY difficult to break through Jupiter's SILENCE BARRIER once it is in place. They prefer to deal with a problem with actions rather than with words. The tendency of Saturn to seize on his every word and want to know What He Meant By It is the best way to send Jupiter back into his shell like a rapidly retreating snail. If she STILL won't leave him alone and goes on questioning him or being deliberately provocative because she WANTS a reaction, he may get angry, and the Snail from Jupiter will come roaring out of his shell and bite her on the ankle (there is nothing worse than an aggressive snail).

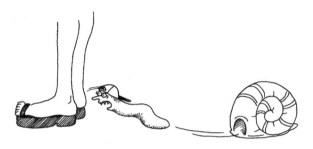

IF YOU PROVOKE HIM, THE SNAIL FROM JUPITER MAY COME ROARING OUT OF HIS SHELL AND BITE YOU ON THE ANKLE.

Interplanetary Disaster Strikes! This happens when Saturn expects Jupiter to talk to her and to listen to her like a fellow inhabitant of Saturn would. She expects him to be fluent in Saturnspeak. He isn't.

The Cosmic Scene

Susie from Saturn: 'James, can I talk to you?'

James from Jupiter: 'Yes, you can. You are. Ha-ha.'

Susie: 'I don't feel like laughing.' (At this point a Best Friend from Saturn would ask, sympathetically, 'What's wrong?' Jupiter, however, interprets the remark, 'I don't feel like laughing,' as a personal challenge. It is an opportunity for him to prove he is irresistibly funny, and

to cheer her up. He MUST make her laugh. So he tells her the one about the nun, the chicken and the banana.)

Susie: 'I SAID I don't feel like laughing! Didn't you hear me?' (Yes, he heard her. But he interpreted the words differently. He is now offended because she didn't laugh at his joke.)

James: 'Hey, don't get stressed with me! What have *I* done?' (The Best Friend from Saturn would try to find out why Saturn was getting upset, and would de-stress her by listening while she talked. Jupiter, on the other hand, takes offence at the fact that she didn't laugh at his joke, and sees her bad mood as a personal attack on HIM. He is now on the defensive. So when she bursts into tears and attempts to cry on his shoulder, he backs away. He cannot handle these sudden changes in mood. As far as he is concerned, she is CROSS with him.)

Susie: 'You don't care about me!'

James: 'I don't know what you mean.' (This is a Statement of Fact.) 'Don't cry. I hate it when you cry.

Here, you can use my handkerchief.' (Jupiter likes to find practical solutions to problems, and this is the only one he can think of. It will do. He feels pleased with himself. She should be all right now.

Susie interprets the offer of the handkerchief as a sign that James really does care about her, and she starts crying and laughing at the same time, out of sheer relief. James is now hopelessly confused, and he edges his way towards the door, planning to escape as soon as possible.)

Susie (*ruefully*): 'This is a revolting handkerchief!' (The Best Friend from Saturn would take this opportunity to have a good laugh with Saturn over something completely silly, such as a revolting handkerchief, before returning, refreshed, to the more serious side of the conversation. Jupiter, however, takes great offence at the fact that she has insulted the only thing he could think to offer her, which was his handkerchief. He is not aware that there *is* a more serious side to the conversation. Insulting his handkerchief is bad enough. As far as he is concerned, if she doesn't like his handkerchief, it means that she doesn't like HIM.)

James: 'Find your own handkerchief, then. I don't care.'

Susie: 'WHAT DO YOU MEAN, YOU DON'T CARE? DON'T YOU CARE ABOUT ME AT ALL??!' (This is an Overreaction from Saturn – more of this later.

James disappears out of the room at high speed.)

The above conversation illustrates that Jupiter and Saturn are Worlds Apart, and that the gulf between them is mainly due to a breakdown in, or lack of, proper communication. James and Susie are talking two different languages. The result is a kind of Interplanetary White Noise, or dense fog of misunderstanding, through which no one can get through to anyone else. They REACT to each other's words instead of UNDERSTANDING.

Strategies For Encouraging Better Communication, Which Leads To Greater Interplanetary Harmony

• Jupiter should learn to listen to Saturn and realise that he doesn't HAVE to offer an instant solution. She will not feel that he is failing her if he does not have everything sorted in the next five minutes. All she wants is to be heard, and to feel that he cares enough to take the time to listen.

• Saturn should realise that Jupiter prefers action to words, and that sitting still and listening presents him with something of a challenge. He may feel the need to bounce a ball up and down at the same time, or do some imaginary football swerves and manoeuvres, or practise a few jumps on his skateboard. This does not mean he doesn't care about her. He is just DIFFERENT. If Saturn wants someone to talk to for hours, it may be A Better Idea if she seeks the company of the Best Friend from Saturn.

• Saturn should be direct but not confrontational when talking to Jupiter. If she keeps hinting that she would like him to take her to a film ('I'd really love to see *Love on a Cold Planet*.' . . . 'Have YOU seen *Love on a Cold Planet*?' . . . 'I've heard that *Love on a Cold Planet* is on at the cinema all this week – I'd really love to see it!'), he may NEVER take the hint, or he may become irritated. It is better if she asks him gently but directly: 'Would you take me to see *Love on a Cold Planet*?' The Wrong Approach is the confrontational one: 'You've known me for six months now and you've NEVER taken me to see a film! Why don't you take me to see *Love on a Cold Planet*?' If her attitude is accusatory and demanding, he will back off at high speed, since she makes him feel as though he is constantly failing. Success, and a sense of achievement, are extremely important to Jupiter.

• Show some appreciation. Even if it's something quite small and insignificant, this can work wonders.

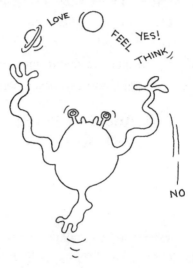

JUGGLING WITH DIFFERENT
WORDS/WORLDS

• Smile! By smiling at each other (and I don't mean a great cheesy grin which makes you look completely mad . . . something a little more subtle will do), Jupiter and Saturn are able to communicate the fact that they like each other, even if they cannot think of anything sensible to say. In fact, smiling, particularly if you smile with your eyes, is a universally recognised sign of friendship (apart from on the planet Zodd, where they raise six legs in greeting and shout, 'Zodd you!', to which the usual response is, 'Zodd it!' Caution: Earthlings are likely to misinterpret these words – so don't try it at home!).

• Sometimes it is better to say NOTHING. Jupiter does not welcome advice or criticism that he did not ask for. A remark such as 'I think you'd look better without the hat' may result in a long-drawn-out Hurt or Injured Silence. Criticism of or advice for Saturn would have to be phrased *very* carefully to avoid interplanetary upset.

• Timing Is Everything! Choose your moment carefully . . .

Good And Bad Moments To Talk To Jupiter

Good Moments

• When he has just achieved something, such as winning a match, passing an exam, performing a spectacular jump on his skateboard, or managing to touch the tip of his nose with his tongue. He will be in A Good Mood.

• When he is on his own, without any of his mates around to tease and embarrass him (and Saturn).

Bad Moments

• When he has just woken up. He should be allowed several hours to get his brain into gear. Saturn should also allow him to finish his meal before she expects him to engage anyone or anything in conversation. He finds it impossible to talk on an empty stomach.

• When he is watching something interesting on television.

• When he is playing a computer game.

BAD TIMES TO TALK TO JUPITER

- When he is trying to think. (Watch out for the slight frown of concentration and the distant look in his eyes.)
- When he is tired.

By now you should be getting the idea that the bad moments to talk to Jupiter far outnumber the good moments. This is only to be expected. He likes space and action, and too many words weigh him down and cramp his style.

Good And Bad Moments To Talk To Saturn

Good Moments

• Any time, day or night, if Jupiter begins his conversation with the words: 'Can I talk to you, please? I really need to talk to someone, and you're the best person I know.' For Jupiter to ask Saturn for help and advice is one of the greatest compliments he can pay her, since it shows that he trusts her enough to let down his guard just for once.

Bad Moments

• When she has just fallen out with the Best Friend from Saturn.

• When she has just made it up with the Best Friend from Saturn, and they are deep in a fascinating and very involved conversation. They will not welcome any interruption.

• When she and the Best Friend from Saturn are giggling uncontrollably (they have gone 'hyper', or are just in a plain silly mood). Jupiter will not get any sense out of her.

Another Good Moment to Talk to Saturn

• When the Best Friend from Saturn is not around. That way Jupiter will not get the uneasy feeling that Saturn and the Best Friend are discussing him as soon as his back is turned.

Finally, the Great Universal Translator has provided some examples of Saturnspeak and Jupiterjargon for the benefit of those who wish to understand their Favourite Alien Being.

Saturnspeak	Translation
'I hate my hair.'	'Please tell me you like my hair.'
'I hate boys.'	'I can't live without them.'
'Have you noticed anything different about me?'	'You have failed to notice I have had highlights put in my hair.'
'What are you thinking?'	'Don't just sit there not saying anything. Talk to me!'

DOES ANYONE NEED A TRANSLATOR? I SPEAK SEVENTY-TWO THOUSAND DIFFERENT LANGUAGES!

'What are you looking at?'

'Why don't you look at me?'

'I think friendship and trust are the most important elements in any relationship.'

'Please kiss me.'

'What's wrong?'

'Tell me about it. I like to be needed.'

'You're a good friend.'

'Thank you for listening.'

Jupiterjargon	Translation
'Girls are OK.'	'Wow! Girls are FANTASTIC!'
'I think you're . . . er . . . you're OK.'	'I love you.'
'Girls? PHWOAR! SEXEEE OR WHAT? WHOOO-HAH!! YEAH!!!'	'I'm terrified of girls.' (But I use a lot of bluff and bluster to cover up my basic insecurity.)
'I don't know what you mean.'	'I don't WANT to know what you mean. Leave me alone. I need some space.'
'Let's go for a cycle-ride/ take the dog for a walk/go or a whiz around the solar system in my spaceship.'	'ANYTHING rather than sit here while you waffle on endlessly . . . I need some ACTION.'

'What's wrong?'

'For God's sake, cheer up or I shall get cross.'

'What's the matter NOW?'

'What have *I* done?'

'You're a good friend.'

'You're fun to be with, and you don't make too many demands on me. Thank you for being there.'

 WORLDS APART

Chapter 2

Worlds Collide

What happens when Worlds Collide and Jupiter crosses with Saturn?

It is the Age of Interplanetary Problems!

Of course, the Boys from Jupiter and the Girls from Saturn have been around for ever, but they never really took much notice of each other. But something has changed . . .

They have started to notice each other a lot more, and, more significantly, they have become aware of the fact that they are being noticed.

This has made some of them quite nervous and excited, while it has completely gone to the heads of others, resulting in a certain amount of strange behaviour in both Jupiter and Saturn.

How Does Saturn's Behaviour Change When She Meets Jupiter?

• She becomes acutely self-conscious and worries about her appearance. She doesn't want Jupiter to be put off by it. This is most unlikely, as long as she is friendly and has a nice smile, but it doesn't stop her worrying. She becomes convinced that Jupiter will laugh at her/fail to notice her altogether, unless she plucks her eyebrows ('They're too bushy, like great hairy Caterpillars from Mars!').

Fact: It is probably not her eyebrows that Jupiter will notice first. Saturn makes the mistake of assuming that he is as aware of minute details of her appearance as she is ('Oh my God, I've got a spot on my left earlobe! He'll never look at me again!'). The fact is, Jupiter is not always *that* observant. Saturn could probably put different shades of colour in her hair every day of the week, and he might not even notice . . .

Samantha from Saturn: 'Have you noticed what colour my hair is?'
Josh from Jupiter: 'Er, yes. It's, er . . . brown. Like it usually is.'

• She becomes very conscious of what she is saying, because she wants to say all the right things to make him like her. Unfortunately, because she is nervous, her brain sometimes refuses to cooperate, and she finds herself saying things like:

'Hi! I'm . . . er . . . I'm, er . . . Oh my God, I've forgotten!'

'Hurggh . . .' (or some other strange noise that comes out of her mouth when what she really wanted to say was, 'How are you?').

• She goes to the other extreme and can't stop talking. Her brain and voice start going at different speeds (both very fast), and she realises she has no control over either of them:

'Hi, I'm Sophie! What's your name? Really? I've got an uncle called Joe. He breeds racing tortoises, no, I

mean turtles, no, sorry, I mean pigeons – must have got them confused with turtle doves, ha-ha. Are you interested in pigeons? No, of course you're not. Silly question. I can see you're not a pigeon sort of person. Oh God, you must think I'm really stupid . . .'

• She says what SHE thinks are stupid things and then, because she feels so embarrassed, she doesn't wait to hear Jupiter's reply.

Sophie from Saturn: 'Do you come here often?' (OH NO, I CANNOT BELIEVE THAT I REALLY *SAID* THAT!)
Joe from Jupiter: 'No. But I will do now.'

This is a nice reply. Unfortunately, Sophie hasn't waited to hear it. Covered in confusion, she has fled to the girls' cloakroom, where she hides for the next half an hour before asking her friends to take her home because she 'doesn't feel very well'.

Fact: Jupiter is probably just as nervous and unsure of himself as Saturn is. He will not be inwardly criticising her every word (and every freckle), because he is rather more concerned about what she thinks of HIM.

Changes In Jupiter's Behaviour Of Which Saturn Should Be Aware

If there is a group of mates in the background, watching him talking to Saturn, the chances are that they have been daring him to go and talk to her ('Go on! Ask her! What are you waiting for? You're not *scared* of her, are

SATURN CAN'T
HELP SMILING, AND
HER EYES SHINE
WHEN JUPITER
WALKS INTO THE
ROOM... (NOTE: JUPITER
MAY ACT COOL IN FRONT OF
HIS MATES, BUT LOOK OUT FOR
THE QUICK SMILE WHICH IS JUST
FOR <u>YOU</u> ...)

you? Go ON!'). This will obviously affect the way he behaves towards her, because he does not want to lose face in front of his friends. He may put on a show of bravado, covering up his basic lack of confidence by being over-loud and over-confident:

Jasper from Jupiter: 'Hi! You're a cool chick. You must be pleased to meet me. WAYYY to go! Crazy. Everybody loves me, babe – wanna join the gang?'

Or he may just stand beside her, not really looking at her, shuffling his feet nervously, and occasionally hissing 'Shut up!' at the sniggering Mates from Jupiter.

The Saturn Guide To Boys' Reactions

Fact: The kind of behaviour described above may make you feel uncomfortable and embarrassed. Try to remember that Jupiter is dealing with a situation that is probably new to him, and he is not out to embarrass you deliberately. He almost certainly wants you to like him, but he feels pulled in two directions. Half of him wants to impress his mates (and be with them), and half of him wants to impress YOU (and be with you). It may take him a while to adjust and to work out that he doesn't have to put on an act. His mates will still like him, and you will still like him, if he behaves in a normal and friendly way.

• He may seem strangely silent and sullen at times. This is not necessarily because he doesn't like you. It may even be because he likes you A LOT. His disgruntled behaviour is probably due to a vague feeling of resentment at being put in a situation where he doesn't know quite what to do or say. His self-esteem will return, and he will cheer up, when he feels more in control of the situation.

First Encounter With An Alien Being (F.A.B.!)

What Saturn and Jupiter Can Do To Make A Meeting Enjoyable:

• Relax. Smile.
• Saturn should stop worrying about whether her make-up has smudged, or whether the spot on her nose has got larger (assuming gigantic proportions, in her imagination!). She should realise that Jupiter himself is not perfect in every detail (he may have a rather noticeable hair growing out of one nostril, or his teeth may be slightly crooked), and she should remember that most boys would find the

Perfect Girl from Saturn quite intimidating (they would naturally assume that she would never be interested in THEM).

• Saturn and Jupiter should ask each other a few gentle questions (not a full-scale interrogation!). They should listen to each other's replies, and not be put off when, after a long pause, they both start speaking at once (this is bound to happen – but it's quite funny).

• They should show an interest in what the other person is talking about. If they find that they have things in common, that's great, but they should remember that the differences are interesting too.

• If Saturn likes Jupiter, she can ask him out. It is OK for Saturn to do this, but she should try not to be too pushy.

The Right Way to Ask Each Other Out: 'Would you like to meet me at that new café in town? I've heard it's really cool.'

The Wrong Way to Ask Each Other Out: 'We MUST meet again. You really OUGHT to go to that great new café in town. Meet me there tomorrow at midday.'

The Right Way is to ask a simple question, leaving each other the option of saying 'no'. The Wrong Way is to tell each other what to do, leaving the other person with the feeling that they have no option, and are being forced into something.

It is OK for Saturn and Jupiter to ask each other out. It is NOT OK to demand, or unfairly pressurise. (Even a small amount of pressure applied to the top of the heads of the inhabitants of the planet Zodd causes them to emit a terrible high-pitched scream and lose all their hair – so don't do it.)

! Interplanetary Problem: First impressions may be wrong impressions

When Jupiter first looks through his telescope at Saturn, she may appear as a cool and distant planet, apparently not interested in him at all. He may even be looking through the wrong end of the telescope and assuming that she is a lot cooler and more distant than she really is. He should bear in mind that he, too, can seem cool and distant in order to hide the fact that he is nervous and unsure of himself. Saturn may be doing the same thing. They both give out the wrong signals in order to protect themselves from looking stupid.

Jordan from Jupiter notices that Sita from Saturn keeps looking at him. But whenever he looks back at her, she looks away quickly. Once, she even frowns at him. He assumes, wrongly, that she doesn't like him.

Interpreting The Signals Correctly

• The fact that Sita keeps looking at him shows that she DOES like him/fancy him. The reason she looks away again quickly is because she is embarrassed that Jordan has noticed her looking at him. The slight frown is for the same reason, because she is worried that he will think

SATURN AND JUPITER
CAN BOTH SEEM LIKE COOL AND
DISTANT PLANETS, WHEN, IN FACT,
THEY ARE BOTH JUST NERVOUS.

she is stupid for repeatedly looking at him. She is also afraid he will think she fancies him. The fact that she really *does* fancy him is beside the point. For him to *know* that she does, makes her vulnerable. What she really wants is for him to be attracted to *her*. Note: Jupiter may feel the same if Saturn notices him looking at her, and she responds by nudging her friends, staring at him and giggling. This makes him feel awkward and vulnerable. She should remember that it is easy to put him off by embarrassing him, and she should avoid doing this if she likes him.

• Jupiter may give misleading signals in order to hide his vulnerability and fear of rejection. He may act super-cool,

DO YOU COME HERE OFTEN?

MELTING THE ICE

uninterested, or he may show off to his mates. Although it can be off-putting if he goes to the other extreme and seems *too* keen, he should remember that Saturn does need some encouragement (a friendly smile will do).

Having interpreted the signals correctly, Jordan should feel encouraged to approach Sita, and talk to her, without worrying that she will be hostile to him. However, he should avoid saying something like: 'I saw you looking at me. Like what you see?'

This instantly puts her on the spot and causes her a double dose of embarrassment, especially if there are other people listening at the time.

Instead, he is more likely to have success if he uses a gentler approach, and asks a question that she can actually answer (as opposed to a clever one at her expense): 'Hi! Mind if I join you? What do you think of this place?'

Once Jupiter and Saturn have got a little closer to each other, they can begin to melt the ice, and they will probably discover that they are both quite warm planets (even RED HOT!). They may begin to warm to each other.

Warning: It produces a pleasant sensation and a warm glow inside when Saturn and Jupiter get close. They may be tempted to melt into each other's arms. But if they get too hot too quickly, Saturn may find that Jupiter starts feeling in need of some fresh air. He needs plenty of space to spin around (on his skateboard, roller blades, bicycle, etc.), and he won't be happy if Saturn collides with him the whole time, and won't leave him alone AT ALL. So she should give him plenty of space, and let him come spinning towards her when he feels ready.

JUPITER IS A <u>BIG</u> PLANET.
HE NEEDS PLENTY OF <u>SPACE</u> ...

Question: How can Jupiter and Saturn collide without striking sparks off each other or getting hurt?

Answer: They should view each other as friends FIRST rather than immediately seeing each other as potential planetary partners in the Greatest Romance Ever To Hit The Universe.

! Interplanetary Problem: Collision-course behaviour

Joe from Jupiter and Sophie from Saturn have now been introduced by A Mutual Friend (and Interplanetary Matchmaker) and they have discovered that they share many interests, including going for long walks and exploring. The following day they go for a walk together and climb a hill to the very top, from where there is a beautiful view. They have been chatting the whole time

GIANT PLUTONIAN GROUND PLODDER

'THESE ARE THE TRACKS OF A GIANT PLUTONIAN GROUND
PLODDER — THEY'RE VERY RARE! WAIT — I'VE FOUND ONE OF
ITS DROPPINGS!'

(although they are slightly out of breath now), and the
conversation has been very friendly, covering all sorts of
subjects from their families to their friends to their mutual
interest in wildlife/birds/animals, etc. Joe is now
explaining the view to Sophie: 'That's Interplanetary
Park over there . . . and you can just see the Astrodome.
Isn't it a wonderful building? Hey! Look down here!' He
gets down on his hands and knees and examines the
ground closely. 'I've found some tracks. I think they've
been made by a Giant Plutonian Ground Plodder. They're
extremely rare, you know. We ought to follow them . . .'
All of a sudden, Sophie, who has been enjoying their
time together enormously up until now, feels a great

surge of dissatisfaction and irritation. It is a beautiful day, the birds are singing, the flowers are blooming, and they are the only two people on top of a hill together, gazing out over a magnificent view. It is a wild and romantic setting. So why doesn't he DO anything wild and romantic? Why doesn't he at least SAY something romantic?

'What's the matter?' asks Joe. 'You don't look very happy.'

'Don't you like me?' replies Sophie.

'What kind of question is that? I don't know what you mean. You were all right just now.'

'Oh it doesn't matter. Forget it! Let's go home.'

'Right. I think I've had enough for one day.'

A small cloud drifts across the sun, a cold breeze starts blowing, and they walk home in an embarrassed and slightly miserable silence.

How To Avoid Collision-Course Behaviour And Become Friends With An Alien Being

First of all, there is nothing wrong with being 'just good friends'. It is important to realise that it isn't a matter of being *just* good friends. Becoming friends with Someone from Another Planet is an important achievement (for which you deserve the Interplanetary Building Bridges Award), and it is likely to be a valuable part of your life. So how do you build your bridges of friendship (as opposed to burning them?).

Use the Universal Language of Friendship. This is understood throughout the galaxy (except on the planet Zodd, where they jump up and down on each other's feet if they want to be friends – the four feet that are still on the ground, that is, since the other six are raised in the air). Here are a few of the basic principles of the Universal Language of Friendship:

HOW TO BE JUST GOOD FRIENDS

SMILE CHEERFULLY...   BUT NOT SEDUCTIVELY...

GIVE A FRIENDLY WINK (PERHAPS NOT...)

DO YOU LIKE ME?   NO!

HI! HOW'S THINGS?   YES!

• Smile cheerfully, but not seductively. (Practise in the mirror if necessary.)

• Don't ask difficult questions. 'Do you like me?' is a challenging and confrontational question, one that implies that the other person is not doing enough to make you feel liked, which is why you have to ask. You are putting pressure on them to give MORE. The most important element in a friendship is that you should both feel RELAXED and not under pressure.

• Use words and expressions such as 'Hi!', 'How are you?', 'It's good to see you!', 'What's new?' and 'Take care!'. All of these are friendly but undemanding. Avoid saying things like 'I've missed you terribly!'. This makes you sound clingy (Clingfilm Syndrome), as though you need the other person to be around all the time or your life isn't worth living. Of course, once your friendship is firmly established, you can have endless fun and say things like, 'I've missed you SOOOOOO much! Come here and give me A BIG KISS!', knowing that the other person won't take you too seriously. But if you do this before the other person has had a chance to get to know you, they may be quite alarmed. They will also feel that you are making fun of them and having a joke at their expense, rather than sharing one with them.

• Don't answer with grunts and 'I don't know'. Try to communicate. It is easy once you get started. Ask questions if you are worried.

A Friendship With An Alien Being should be built on the four pillars of ACCEPTING and RESPECTING, SHARING and CARING. You accept that they are different

RESPECT!   ACCEPT!

from you (their attitude and their outlook are different), you respect the differences between you and don't try to change them, you share your interests and experiences in a light-hearted and straightforward manner, and you care about the other person from a respectful distance, without invading their space. If they need you (or vice versa), they know that you are there for them. BEING THERE is very important. It may not be necessary, or even desirable, to see each other every single day, or to talk too much (you run the risk of your friendship getting bogged down in a conversation containing too many heavy words – so keep it light), as long as you know that the other person is out there somewhere.

Interplanetary Advice To Saturn

Don't turn to Your Friend from Jupiter every time you have a problem or need a shoulder to cry on. It is OK to do this once or twice (and Jupiter should accept that it is a sign that you trust him and look on him as A Good Friend), but remember that he is different, and that he

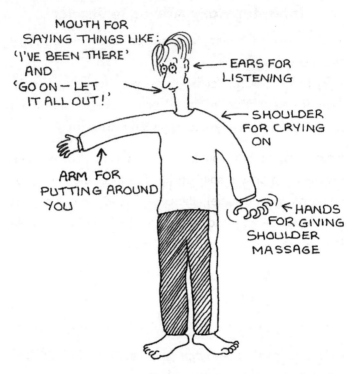

MOUTH FOR SAYING THINGS LIKE: 'I'VE BEEN THERE' AND 'GO ON – LET IT ALL OUT!'

EARS FOR LISTENING

SHOULDER FOR CRYING ON

ARM FOR PUTTING AROUND YOU

HANDS FOR GIVING SHOULDER MASSAGE

THE BEST FRIEND FROM SATURN

finds it hard enough to deal with his own emotions, let alone those of a weeping Saturn. Even if he is a New Age Guy and keen on getting in touch with his emotions, he may not be *that* keen to get in touch with *yours*.

At moments of drama and crisis in your life, when you need someone to listen to you and hold your hand (particularly if these moments occur on average more than six times a week), you may be better advised to turn to the Best Friend from Saturn.

Interplanetary Advice To Jupiter

• Don't expect Saturn to share all your interests. Try sharing some of hers.

• Try to trust Saturn. You'll find her very helpful in a crisis. Also, if you confide in her at such a time, it will be the greatest compliment you can give her as a friend.

Note to Saturn: If you have a practical problem that requires a practical solution (for instance, the chain has come off your bicycle), then the Friend from Jupiter is Your Man! He will usually enjoy the feeling of being able to offer you help in a positive and practical way.

How Friends Can Affect
The Way You See Each Other

! Interplanetary Problem: Friends who talk too much

There is Saturn with her telescope, admiring another

ANOTHER HEAVENLY BODY APPROACHES
IN HIS SUPER-COOL MINI SPACE POD

Heavenly Body from Jupiter just floating into her field of vision in his super-cool mini Space Pod (great little space-ships for going for a quick spin around the galaxy), when a Friend from Saturn suddenly grabs the telescope out of her trembling hands and looks through it.

'Oh God, what a creep!' she exclaims.

'Do you mean the one in the Space Pod?'

'Yes. He's awful.'

'I thought he was rather cute.'

'Cute? Cute he is NOT. His eyes are too close together. It's a sign of meanness, you know. That's what I've heard. Siobhan from Saturn said she was told by Sadie from Saturn who was told by Someone from Saturn, that he pulled all the legs off a Scarlet Silk Spider from Saturn (it took a long time because it had more than three thousand legs), and then he trod on it. And all this vile scarlet stuff came out . . .'

'Oh GROSS!'

'Exactly. So you don't want to have anything to do with HIM.'

Yes. Friends can Put You Off. RIGHT OFF.

SCARLET SILK SPIDER FROM SATURN

60

But wait a minute. There may be something that Friend from Saturn has forgotten to mention. Such as the fact that she really fancies the Heavenly Body in the Space Pod, and that last Friday she got all dressed up and went to a lot of trouble with her appearance and then asked him out. And he said no. And he didn't say anything else. So she feels hurt, rejected and humiliated. It would be the final straw, as far as she is concerned, if her Friend from Saturn and the Heavenly Body were to get together. That is why she is saying everything she possibly can to put her off.

Interplanetary Advice: Saturn and Jupiter should bear in mind that a friend's view of someone they like may be coloured by their own feelings and experiences. It is better to meet the person, talk to them and decide for themselves. They should not be put off by other people's opinions, especially if they are based on hearsay.

Similarly, Saturn should not allow herself to be too heavily influenced by the Matchmaker from Saturn. She will tell her that there is a WONDERFUL boy who is dying to meet her. She will try to convince her that she and he are destined to fall in love. If Saturn lets herself be persuaded that this is true, she may be in for a terrible disappointment when he turns out to be not her type at all.

Of course, friends need not necessarily distort the image of the Alien Being. They can even help you to see more clearly (sometimes by wiping just a few of the stars out of your eyes).

How The Best Friend From Saturn Helps Saturn To Gain A More Balanced View Of The Godlike Creature On Whom She Has Set Her Sights

Sita from Saturn: 'Sarah! Look! It's HIM! Isn't he just WONDERFUL? Hasn't he got THE most AMAZING body? Oh my God, he looked at me! Sarah! He LOOKED at me!!! What am I going to do? Do I look OK, or do I look completely stupid? My ears are too big, aren't they? He probably thinks I'm related to an elephant. He'll never look at me again. No boy will, except to have a good laugh. Oh NO. He's going away . . . He HATES me! WHY??! Oh, come BACK! Pleeeeeeease come back . . . !'

Interplanetary Advice: DON'T PANIC! Instead, Saturn should go straight to the Best Friend from Saturn and she will drop pearls of wisdom in Saturn's ear (which is quite a normal size, really).

STAR – STRUCK

Wise Words Uttered by Best Friend from Saturn

'Calm down!'

Morale-Boosting Words Uttered by Best Friend from Saturn

'Of COURSE he doesn't hate you! He doesn't even know you. If he did, I know he'd really like you. And if he didn't like you, there'd be something wrong with him, and he wouldn't be worth bothering with anyway, because you're a really beautiful person. And your ears aren't THAT big. In fact, you're lucky, because you've got room for HEAPS of earrings . . .'

Words of Caution Uttered by Best Friend from Saturn

'I've heard that he asked the Sister of Sally from Saturn out, and he never showed up. And he never said sorry, either. So don't raise your hopes too high in case he lets you down.'

If Saturn takes all these Wise Words on board, she will start to feel calmer, steadier and more focused. This is a good feeling, but it doesn't always last very long (it lasts until the next time HE walks past . . .).

Who Needs Friends? (You Do!)

There is an ancient Earth Saying: 'Two's company; three's a crowd.' There are times when it may be preferable to be in a crowd (of at least three), since it is a lot

FRIENDS CAN HELP YOU TO RELAX

easier to view Alien Beings when you have the support and company of friends from Your Own Planet. There are also MORE Heavenly Bodies to view (including the Friend of the Friend of the Brother of Jupiter, who is introduced to you by the Friend of the Friend of the Sister of Saturn, etc., etc.). Your friends give you confidence, and you can have a laugh with them, which helps you to relax (as opposed to standing there on your own, feeling intensely self-conscious, not daring to move in case your shoes creak and people LOOK at you). Being part of a group gives both Saturn and Jupiter the opportunity to direct swift glances at each other and to compare notes and impressions with their friends before committing themselves to A Closer Encounter.

! Interplanetary Problem: The closer encounter

Samantha from Saturn: 'Hurrgh . . . I mean, hello! I was just wondering . . . er . . . if you would like to meet after school one day. We could go for a walk or something.'

Josh from Jupiter: 'Er . . .'

Samantha: 'It doesn't matter. Really.'

Josh: 'No! I mean, yes! Er, that is . . . I think so.'

Samantha: 'Er . . . which?'

Josh: 'Er . . . what?'

Samantha: 'Could you just make up your mind?'

Josh: 'Oh! Er . . . yes, of course! That'd be great. I think.'

Samantha: 'Cool.'

ER, I WAS WONDERING, ER... SHUT UP! ...IF YOU, ER...

GO ON, JOSH — ASK HER!

THE CLOSER ENCOUNTER

Understanding Each Other's Reactions And How To Handle A Closer Encounter

• Jupiter uses fewer words than Saturn. When he says to her, 'Er . . . um . . . er . . . hi!', it means, 'It's really great to meet you!' If he tends to mumble, or avoid meeting her eye, it is not because he doesn't really want to talk to her or look at her. It is probably because he is nervous and is aware that the Mates from Jupiter are all watching him. Jupiterjargon is a language of understatement, and a great deal of meaning can be condensed into a few, brief words. 'Er . . . I think you're OK,' may mean, 'Wow! You're fantastic! I love you! I can't live without you!'

• Saturnspeak, on the other hand, tends to be a full and flowery language, expansive and exuberant, and totally O.T.T. at times. Jupiter may be puzzled when she comes over to him and starts waffling about her pet tortoise, and how she is planning to become a nuclear scientist, and isn't it a hot day, and does he like Interplanetary Techno-Jazz? Why on earth (or Why By Jupiter) is she telling him all these things, or asking him all these questions? She is just rambling on and on, and there seems to be no point to all the waffle.

What Jupiter needs to remember: The fact that she is talking to him at all is significant. The meaning behind all the apparently inconsequential words is likely to be: 'I like you.' All he needs to do is listen.

• Saturn should avoid waffling on for more than half an hour without taking a breath. Almost anyone is likely to lose interest if you don't give them a chance to speak.

• Saturn appreciates eye contact. If Jupiter looks at her while she is talking, or while he is talking, it shows he is interested. He should certainly avoid looking around the room and giving out signals to other passing Saturns while he is talking to HER. This is most unfair, and likely to make her nervous and ill at ease, even angry.

• Jupiter should be aware that he can also overdo the eye contact. Just because he is with the Mates from

'YOU ARE THE BRIGHTEST STAR THAT SHINES IN MY UNIVERSE! SHALL I COMPARE THEE TO AN AUGUST BANK HOLIDAY — THOU ART MORE WONDROUS...'

DON'T EXPECT JUPITER TO WAFFLE ON LIKE THIS...

'I, ER, I THINK ...ER...YOU'RE O.K.!'

HE TENDS TO SAY <u>MORE</u> WITH FEWER WORDS.

Jupiter, he should not feel it is OK to stare hard at Someone from Saturn and deliberately try to embarrass her.

• Both Saturn and Jupiter should remember that a warm smile is the best way to melt the ice.

MESSENGER FROM JUPITER

BEWARE OF FALSE MESSENGERS

Chapter 3

The Date

Pre-Date Tension: How To Handle It

Preparing to go out for the first time with someone you really like is an exciting and nerve-racking time. (Will they like what you're wearing? Will you say the right things to make them like you? Will they even turn up?) If you are a seething mass of insecurities, what do you do?

Saturn will usually turn to the Best Friend from Saturn for help and advice (or just to listen while she talks about HIM and expresses her feelings – this helps to relieve the nervous pressure building up inside). Saturn SHARES the whole experience from start to finish.

Jupiter pretends he is FINE. He may brag a little to the Mates from Jupiter about the impending date, but he has no wish to share his insecurities. He wants the world (and the whole Universe, particularly Saturn) to think he is cool, confident and in control.

Because he usually lacks the support of an under-standing friend who will reassure him, he is more likely

WELL, IT WAS ALL WORTH IT! YOU LOOK <u>FANTASTIC</u>! HE'S JUST GOING TO <u>LOVE</u> YOU!

RUSTLE

RUSTLE

HAIR DYE

SHOPPINGDROME

SATURN HAS PLENTY OF HELP AND ADVICE FROM HER BEST FRIEND WHEN PREPARING FOR A DATE.

suddenly to get cold feet at the last moment and to back out of the whole thing. This is most unfair on Saturn (who has spent the last four days getting ready), but she should try to understand that Jupiter is out there On His Own, emotionally (it may be a self-imposed aloneness, but it is part of what makes him different). He may make a really stupid excuse why he can't meet you, but, if you want him to ask you out on another occasion, it is better to accept his excuse and gently encourage him to try again. If you get angry, he will retreat into his shell, and THAT WILL BE THAT. The Greatest Love In The Universe That Never Was.

When Jupiter Or Saturn Pulls Out

The Cosmic Scene

Jordan from Jupiter: 'Er . . . look . . . er, I'm really sorry about this, but . . . er, I've got to mow the grass this afternoon. Mum says I've got to. So I won't be able to meet you.'

Sita from Saturn: 'But it won't take you THAT long! How much grass have you got? A huge great park or something?' (Picking holes in his argument and making fun of him will NOT go down well, and you should resist the urge to do so, no matter how annoyed you are.)

Jordan: 'Look, I just can't make it. OK?'

Sita: 'No, it's NOT OK. I've just spent four hours' – days, actually – 'getting ready, and you let me down at the last minute, and it's just NOT ON.'

She slams down the phone/marches off with her nose in the air (and then immediately wishes she hadn't behaved like this, because it is difficult to face someone again after you have lost your temper with them – and she still likes him).

Right Way to React When Jupiter Pulls Out of a Date

Jordan from Jupiter: 'Er . . . look . . . er, I'm really sorry about this, but . . . er, I've just been asked to go down the deepest pothole on Pluto this afternoon, and it's a once-in-a-lifetime opportunity because the pothole is open only once in a purple Plutonian moon, and I won't be asked again and I, er . . . I, er . . .'

STRAIGHT DOWN A PLUTONIAN
POTHOLE

Sita from Saturn: 'Look, it's OK. I don't mind. You go down your pothole' – she should resist saying, 'And I hope you never come out of it again' – 'and have a great time. I'll see you some time, I hope.'

This is gentle but encouraging and lets him off the hook. He will realise that you are a relaxed and friendly individual, and this will make it more likely that he will ask you out on another occasion.

Wrong Way To React When Saturn Pulls Out The Cosmic Scene

Jezir from Jupiter: 'I'll see you tonight!'

Sally from Saturn: 'No, I don't think you will. I'm really sorry, but my mum's making me stay in. She thinks I'm looking tired.'

Jezir: 'Oh. Well, how about tomorrow? Or any evening?'

Sally: 'Sorry. I expect I'll still be tired.'

Jezir: 'You don't look tired to me.'

Sally: 'Well, I *am*. And my mum has noticed. At least she cares.'

Jezir: 'And I don't? Suit yourself. I'll see you some time.'

Jezir has sensed that Sally is not keen to go out with him, and is making excuses. He covers up his fear of rejection by becoming offhand to the point of rudeness. Unfortunately, this is likely to put Sally off even more.

Right Way to React When Saturn Pulls Out

Sally: 'I'm sorry, Jezir. I'm really tired, so I'm going to get an early night.'

Jezir: 'Look, it's OK. Don't worry. Get some rest. Maybe see you when you're feeling better? 'This time Jezir avoids questioning Sally and putting pressure on her, which is likely to provoke an angry reaction from Saturn. He shows consideration for her feelings, and the fact that she is tired, but also encourages her to get in touch when she wants to.

! Interplanetary Warning: Always tell the other person if you are not going to turn up. Standing someone up is a very unkind thing to do. (Imagine how you would feel.)

Assuming that no one is planning to pull out or cancel (your date with Jupiter/Saturn is GO!), how do Jupiter and Saturn prepare themselves for the great occasion?

! Interplanetary Problem: What to say

This may be more of a problem for Jupiter. In Saturn's case, it is more likely to be a matter of what NOT to say and how to stop herself from gabbling like an idiot (due to nerves). Of course, she may be just as tongue-tied as Jupiter, in which case An Awkward Silence may result.

THE AWKWARD SILENCE...

THIS IS USUALLY PUNCTUATED BY CLEARING OF THE THROAT AND A VERY <u>LOUD</u> TUMMY RUMBLE...

Advice To Jupiter And Saturn

It is the fear of this Awkward Silence which may even cause you to get cold feet and call the whole thing off. If you are particularly worried that you will lose the power of speech when you are in the sole company of the Person from the Other Planet, it may be better to take a friend with you or to go out on a joint date or as part of a crowd. Alternatively here's:

How to Break the Interplanetary Ice

• Crack a stupid joke. It doesn't matter *how* stupid. It will give you both an excuse to laugh, which will break the

Awkward Silence. (If he/she doesn't laugh, but just stares at you as though you are mad, is he/she worth it?)

• Play some music. LOUDLY.

• Admit to having run out of things to say. Show you're human, rather than desperately trying to impress. Admitting to being human and fallible makes both Saturn and Jupiter more sympathetic and approachable, although Saturn may find it easier than Jupiter to admit to having faults.

LAUGHING HELPS (AS LONG AS IT IS NOT TOO FORCED)

• Saturn should NOT say things like: 'You're really shy, aren't you?' Jupiter will interpret this as a criticism, not as a sign that she likes him (which is the correct interpretation).

A Final Word of Interplanetary Advice

Both Saturn and Jupiter should avoid the temptation to rehearse in advance what they are going to say. If you do this, it will inevitably sound stilted and unnatural (rather like: 'I . . . am . . . an . . . A-L-I-E-N . . .'), and the words may even come out in the wrong order:

HOW SATURN REACTS WHEN JUPITER TELLS A JOKE.

SHE FANCIES HIM

SHE'S JEALOUS

SHE WILL START LAUGHING FIVE MINUTES LATER WHEN SOMEONE HAS EXPLAINED THE JOKE TO HER.

HOW JUPITER REACTS WHEN SATURN TELLS A JOKE.

OH, YEAH —THAT'S REALLY, ER ...FUNNY...

THEY REACT LIKE THIS BECAUSE 'GIRLS ARE NO GOOD AT TELLING JOKES' (BUT THEY HAVE A SNEAKING SUSPICION THAT HER JOKE WAS FUNNIER THAN ANY OF THEIRS. THEY ALSO SUSPECT HER OF HAVING A JOKE AT THEIR EXPENSE).

Jordan from Jupiter: 'It is such a pleasure to eat you, Sita. Would you care for something to see?'

! Interplanetary Problem: Where to go

Points to Consider When Planning Where to Go

• Find out what you can about the other person's interests. Check if the place or activity you have in mind is likely to meet with their approval. (For example, if Saturn is terrified of spiders, it is probably not a good idea for

Jupiter to take her to see *Revenge Of The Killer Silk Spiders*, no matter how much he has been longing to see it.)

• Even if Saturn is dying to show him off to her friends and family, it is a daunting prospect for Jupiter to be introduced to Mr and Mrs Saturn or plunged into the centre of a giggling and whispering circle of Sisters from Saturn on a first date. It is better to find some neutral spot away from both the Saturn and Jupiter homeworlds, where you can relax and chat at your ease.

Final Points To Consider Before
The Great Interplanetary Date

• Both Saturn and Jupiter should try to prevent their imaginations going into hyperdrive and painting pictures of all sorts of blissful and wonderful things (or even disastrous and panic-inducing situations) which may never happen. If you paint an over-rosy picture in your mind, you may end up feeling disappointed and dissatisfied with the reality of the situation. And if you think of all the things that could go wrong, you will be a gibbering nervous wreck by the time the great day arrives.

• Jupiter should make sure he is on time for a date. If he is late, Saturn will have started worrying that he is not going to turn up, and she is likely to be more tense than she would otherwise have been. If he is early (which is less likely), she will be in the middle of her final preparations, and will probably smudge mascara all over her face in her haste to get ready. Again, she will not be as relaxed as she would otherwise have been, had she been given the extra few minutes she needed.

• Relax. Take a deep breath. Remember to breathe out again. The great moment has arrived . . . Jupiter crosses with Saturn, and fate takes them on a date together . . .

ENJOY!

The Great Interplanetary Date

Jezir from Jupiter and Sally from Saturn go to the cinema together.

How did they meet? Jezir from Jupiter was introduced to Sally from Saturn by the Friend of the Friend of the Sister of Joe from Jupiter who is going out with Sophie from Saturn, who is Sally's Best Friend. (Have you got that?)

Which film do they go to? They go to see *Love on a Cold Planet*.

What happens? They sit in the back row because they have heard that all sorts of exciting things happen when you sit in the back row at the cinema. (Not that either of

SALLY AND JEZIR SIT SIDE BY SIDE IN THE BACK ROW AT THE CINEMA

HE TRIES TO HOLD HER HAND,
BUT THE FILM IS VERY SAD, AND
SHE IS TOO BUSY BLOWING HER NOSE.

them actually mentions this – they just go and sit there, without saying anything very much.)

What happens next? They sit there, side by side, acutely aware of each other but not looking at each other or saying anything. The awful possibility of An Awkward Silence looms, until Jezir, in a sudden fit of inspiration, says: 'Would you like some popcorn?' Sally replies: 'No, thank you. I don't like it.' Then some adverts start showing on the screen. They both inwardly heave a sigh of relief, and watch an advert for a local Indian restaurant as if it is the most fascinating thing they have ever seen.

The film begins *Love on a Cold Planet* is all about two star-crossed lovers, and it is very sad and moving and has a tragic ending. Sally imagines herself and Jezir as the two star-crossed lovers and cries most of the way through the film.

Jezir makes one or two attempts to hold her hand, but each time he finds she is busy burrowing in her bag searching for another tissue to blow her nose. So he gives up.

The film ends They leave. Sally's eyes are red-rimmed from weeping, her nose is red from the emotion of it all, and she looks exhausted. Jezir is quite worried by her appearance. 'Are you all right?' he asks. 'Didn't you like the film?'

'Oh yes!' exclaims Sally. 'It was WONDERFUL! I enjoyed every minute. I haven't cried so much for ages!'

'I thought it was a load of rubbish,' says Jezir, feeling slightly irritated. As far as he is concerned, the back row in the cinema is overrated. Sally feels disappointed at his unromantic attitude.

On the way home they stop at MacDoodah's for something to eat.

'Would you like a Jumboburger from Jupiter,' asks Jezir, 'or a Savoury Sausage Sandwich from Saturn?'

'I'm not hungry. I'll have a Coke.'

Instead of eating, she starts talking about the problems she is having at home (she doesn't get on with her step-father, her mother is always working and never has any time to listen, and the dog has a severe wind problem which is making the atmosphere at home even worse, and . . .).

'You're not listening!' she exclaims. 'You're reading the menu!'

'Er, sorry!' Jezir apologises. 'What were you saying?'

'It doesn't matter.'

Please note: When Saturn says, 'It doesn't matter,' she usually means, 'It DOES matter.'

They leave MacDoodah's and decide to part company. They have both had ENOUGH (and I am not referring to the enormous Jumboburger from Jupiter).

Tips For Ensuring That Your Date Really IS Great

• If you are plagued by Awkward Silences, going to a film, concert or disco is quite a good idea, since the film/music/dancing provides a distraction, and the noise drowns out any awkward gaps in the conversation. In fact, conversation may be quite impossible, which is sometimes a great relief.

• On the other hand, if you would prefer to have a quiet chat, go for a walk in the park or visit the local museum if it is raining. (Walking in the rain can be romantic, although a light drizzle may be preferable to a torrential downpour.) If you want a *very* quiet chat, visit your local library.

• Go round the shops if you feel like it, but Saturn shouldn't expect Jupiter to wait endlessly in boutiques (or just outside them) while she spends hours in the changing-rooms trying on heaps of clothes. She should avoid asking him questions such as: 'Does my bottom look big in this?' (What does she expect him to say?) This sort of thing is better done in the company of the Best Friend from Saturn.

• If he would prefer Saturn not to cry all over him, Jupiter should avoid taking her to a weepy film. He should try a comedy instead (such as *Zany Antics on the Planet Zodd*). Laughter unites Jupiter and Saturn, whereas Jupiter finds Saturn's tears rather challenging, since crying is something he has been discouraged from doing since early childhood.

• Saturn should not expect Jupiter to eat and concentrate his full attention on what she is saying at the same time. If his attention wanders, she should not be too quick to take offence, especially if she is talking about problems and traumas in her own life. It is better to keep the conversation light and breezy on a first date rather than getting too heavy. It is also friendly to share a meal rather

 than refuse everything and to sit and watch someone while they are eating. (Order a light Saturn Salad Snack if you are trying to eat healthily.)

THEY GAZE INTO
EACH OTHER'S EYES.
WORDS AREN'T NECESSARY...

WOW! THIS IS
AMAZING!
I MEAN, YOU
AND ME! WOW!
I CAN'T WAIT TO
TELL SARAH...

... BUT SATURN USUALLY MANAGES TO
THINK OF A FEW.

• Finally, Jupiter and Saturn should show by their body language (by smiling, and meeting each other's eyes) that they like each other and they have enjoyed themselves. If they stare at their feet, or at a nearby lamppost, the other person will assume that they are not interested. Jupiter should also be aware that if Saturn lingers and seems unwilling to say goodbye, she is probably waiting for him to ask her out again, and he should feel encouraged to do so, even if she seems a little cool and distant. The ice is just beginning to melt . . .

Not-So-Great Interplanetary Date: The Bad Date

Jordan from Jupiter goes into town with Sita from Saturn.

The wrong place to go: Jordan takes Sita to his favourite café, where he usually hangs out with his Mates from Jupiter. They are all there, as usual. Apart from calling out something like, 'Oh look, here's Jordy with his GIRL-FRIEND!' and giving a few laddish whistles and whoops, which makes Sita feel uncomfortable (she is not sure yet if she really is Jordan's girlfriend), they all immediately start chatting among themselves, and Sita is left sitting, staring into her Coke, ignored by them all.

Wrong thing to say: When they leave the café Jordan says to Sita: 'My mates are great, aren't they? Have you had a good time?' Sita replies: 'No.' (It would seem to be 'no' in answer to *both* questions.)

Wrong thing to do: Part company in a moody silence.

What to do when things don't work out: If Saturn and Jupiter really like each other, but the date was a disaster, they should not assume that they have messed up completely. DON'T DESPAIR.

Helpful Hints On Handling Difficult Dates

• Learn from your mistakes. The Girl from Saturn will find this easier to do than the Boy from Jupiter, who finds it harder to admit, to anyone apart from himself, that he has made any mistakes or has any faults. So Saturn may have to put things right for both of them. This is not as hard as it sounds – she should simply steer him gently in the right direction.

• When Jupiter asks Saturn whether she liked the Mates from Jupiter, and if she had a good time, she should grit her teeth (not too noticeably) and say 'yes'. What's the point of upsetting him? He has taken her to one of his favourite places and introduced her to his favourite friends. This was meant as a compliment, as he was sharing part of his life – an important part – with her. She should take it as a compliment and leave it at that.

• She should smile and suggest that they go somewhere nice that SHE knows of. (But she should not take him any-where she'll end up gossiping and giggling with *her* mates, leaving him out of it.) Jupiter and Saturn should choose a neutral spot where they can talk (or at least admire the view).

Bad Things To Say On A First Date

• 'This is where I bring all my girlfriends.'

• 'This is the first time I've been out with someone shorter than myself!' (This may be a simple statement of fact, but Jupiter will take it as a criticism.)

• 'I saw you the other day shopping with your mum.' (Jupiter does not wish to be reminded of this – he wants to feel cool, confident and in control, and going shopping with his mum falls firmly into the category of 'uncool'.)

- 'I'm bored.'
- 'I really fancy your friend Sarah. Will you introduce me to her?'
- 'My whole life's a mess. God, I'm so depressed! Nothing nice EVER happens to me. Mind if I cry all over you?'

Chapter 4

Falling in Love

How To Handle Falling In Love With An Alien Being

What happens: Susie from Saturn falls in love with James from Jupiter. Their eyes meet across a crowded classroom. (They may have seen each other before but SUDDENLY they see each other DIFFERENTLY, as Heavenly Bodies or Divine Beings to whom they feel a super-charged magnetic attraction.) Romantic music wells up out of nowhere, and heavenly harmonies are heard, but with one or two discords . . .

The Likely Effect Of Falling In Love On Saturn and Jupiter

• She can't take her eyes off him. He can't take his eyes off her.
• They want to be together the whole time.
• They want each other's undivided attention.

THEIR EYES MEET ACROSS A CROWDED CLASSROOM ...

• They find it hard to concentrate, and float around in a kind of daydream, causing a mixture of amusement and annoyance to the Interplanetary Parents.

• They become moody and have difficulty sleeping.

• Saturn spends even more time on the phone than usual.

• Jupiter becomes even less communicative than usual, only managing the odd grunt in response to parental questions ('Are you all right?').

They are flattered by each other's attentions, but they may begin to feel suffocated if they sense that the other person is unwilling to leave them alone for one minute (Clingfilm Syndrome).

Interplanetary Advice

• Jupiter and Saturn should avoid pushing the situation. It is a good idea to give each other space.

• When Saturn turns away from him, Jupiter may think she is deliberately ignoring him, and turning her back on him – when, in reality, she is just trying to get on with her work. It is offputting to both Jupiter and Saturn to be questioned about their every move.

• It is better for Saturn to turn to the Best Friend from Saturn for reassurance, rather than blurting out her insecurities to Jupiter himself. (While he would be happy enough to meet her in the school cafeteria for a Coke and a friendly chat, he probably doesn't appreciate being trapped in the corridor for the whole of morning break while she rambles on endlessly about the hopelessness of everything, especially of her love for him . . .)

• She should beware of firing off angry letters in the heat of the moment (she has seen him chatting up Someone Else from Saturn, and she is jealous). Writing down her deepest feelings in a letter to Jupiter makes her even more vulnerable. (What if he turns out to be unkind, and shows her letter to the Mates from Jupiter? How will she ever live it down?) She should ask herself if she would actually *say* to his face the things she has written.

• Instead of writing letters, Jupiter and Saturn could try

writing everything down in a diary or journal. This is usually therapeutic.

• They should stop trying to understand why love is so confusing, and just accept that it is. It is important to ACCEPT what you cannot change, and to treat each other with RESPECT. Saturn may have to accept the fact that Jupiter is not the best listener in the universe. He needs space and action. But Jupiter should also accept that sometimes she needs to talk. He should avoid saying things like 'Oh for heaven's sake, you do GO ON!' He has no more right to criticise her for talking or expressing her feelings than she has a right to criticise him for wanting to go off and play football or ride his bike. Saturn and Jupiter are both free spirits, and the quickest way to ruin a relationship is to attempt to change the other person.

AVOID HEAD–ON CONFRONTATION

Strategies For Survival When Jupiter Crosses With Saturn And Worlds Collide

• Jupiter and Saturn should avoid head-on confrontation. (Instead of demanding, 'Do you love me?', they should try saying, 'I really like you', and leave each other to respond if and when they want to.)

• They can encourage each other's friendship by show-ing that they are easy to get on with, and fun.

• They should smile and have a good laugh. (If Saturn feels like crying, she should go and see the Best Friend from Saturn.)

• Jupiter and Saturn should learn to revolve peacefully around each other, creating gentle waves of Interplanetary Harmony, which will spread out across the universe . . .

• Remember the key words ACCEPT and RESPECT.

Worlds In Harmony
(Or What Happens When Saturn And Jupiter Have Become An Interplanetary Item)

The tumultuous Overture of First Love (played by the com-bined Orchestras of Saturn and Jupiter) has now settled down to a quieter and gentler pace, with occasional stormy and dramatic passages, followed by sweet and sad little melodies played (usually) by the Soloist from Saturn. Then the Heavenly Harmonies are heard again, although some of the Cosmic Musicians are finding that they need to tune their instruments, which have gone a little flat.

If you are wondering what all this means, let me put it another way. Sophie from Saturn is going out with Joe from Jupiter, Susie from Saturn is going steady with James from Jupiter, Jordan from Jupiter is dating Sita from Saturn, Josh from Jupiter is going out with Samantha from Saturn, and Jezir from Jupiter has been seeing Sally from Saturn for over three months! They are all in long-term (especially the summer term, when they see each other every day at school) relationships, and they are having to deal with the problems that arise when you are in such a relationship.

! Interplanetary Problem: Going a little flat

The Cosmic Scene (1): Sophie and Joe had their first kiss on top of their favourite hill as the sun set slowly over Universal Valley and its last flickering rays shone on the mighty Astrodome in the middle of Interplanetary Park. It was a truly spectacular moment, and the Great Universal Orchestra played the Overture of First Love furiously for the next seven or eight days. Sophie and Joe held hands, gazed into each other's eyes and could think of nothing else except each other. Aaaaah . . .

Until . . . Sophie walks into the classroom on the ninth morning of their relationship and finds Joe sitting on his own at a table, working.

Sophie: 'Joe! There you are! I've been looking for you. I haven't seen you for half an hour. Are you avoiding me? I've missed you terribly!'
Joe: 'Er, I've got some work to do. I seem to have got a bit behind for some reason. I've got to catch up.'
Sophie: 'Why won't you look at me? What's wrong?'
Joe: 'Nothing's wrong!'

INTERPLANETARY PAIRS

JORDAN AND SITA

SAMANTHA AND JOSH

SUSIE AND JAMES

SOPHIE AND JOE

JEZIR AND SALLY

SYBIL AND JEREMY

TOGETHER ... NO MATTER WHAT WEATHER ...

Sophie: 'So. Work is more important to you than our relationship, is it? Well, thanks a lot!'

She turns and storms out of the room.

THE SLOB FROM JUPITER

WHAT'S UP, SUZE?

The Cosmic Scene (2): In another part of the school, Susie from Saturn is standing disconsolately in a doorway, watching the Love of her Life (James from Jupiter), who is sitting with his legs propped up on a desk, chatting with the Mates from Jupiter. He calls out to her: 'Hi, Suse! What's up?'

'Nothing much.'

'Something is. You don't seem very happy.'

'It doesn't matter.'

James is sufficiently fluent in Saturnspeak to know that whatever it is that is bothering Susie DOES matter, but he can't imagine what this might be. He finds her moods difficult to cope with because she doesn't tell him what is wrong, but seems to expect him to guess. He finds himself feeling irritated that there is (apparently) something wrong. Is it something he said/didn't say/did/didn't do? His mind begins to go round in circles, and he wonders why their relationship can't just be fun. He finds her a lot more attractive when she smiles! So when he asks her again, 'What's wrong?', he sounds cross and resentful. He is not necessarily cross with Susie, but frustrated by his own inability to deal with the situation. Inevitably, Susie interprets his crossness as a lack of caring, and they argue.

Interplanetary Advice

• It is best to communicate. If there is a real problem, it is a good idea to tell the other person rather than leaving them to worry that it's their fault or to try to guess what's wrong.

• If there isn't a real problem, but you're just in a foul mood (a bad hair day, perhaps, or an annoying insect bite behind your left knee, which isn't helping), it would be a very good idea to leave the other person alone rather than take out your bad feelings on them. (Go and annoy an inhabitant of the planet Zodd instead. You could be some time because Zoddites never get angry.)

James asks himself why the MAGIC has gone out of their relationship. Or has it?

There are certain steps both Saturn and Jupiter can take to keep the magic alive, as the next chapter shows.

Chapter 5

Keeping a Good Thing Going

Hints On How To Keep The Fires On Saturn And Jupiter Burning

• Both Jupiter and Saturn should make some time for Other Things and Other People (some of their other friendships have, perhaps, been neglected recently). They will realise that they each have more going on in their lives than just each other, and they are likely to find each other more interesting as a result.

• They should try not to take everything personally, and should remember that they tend to think and react in different ways. (Occasionally it may seem to Saturn that Jupiter does not think *at all!*) Jupiter tends to throw himself into activities that take his mind OFF things, whereas Saturn has a tendency to BROOD. Saturn's involved thought processes are often a mystery to Jupiter.

• Jupiter and Saturn both need reassurance from time to time that they both still care about each other. This reassurance can be given verbally ('You're really special!') or in the form of a little gift (it doesn't need to be anything

very much – perhaps something made in an art class), as a symbol of the friendship that exists.

Note to encourage heavenly harmony: Jupiter and Saturn should both be aware that it is unrealistic to expect the initial flush of excitement when they first met to last for ever (even if it feels, at the time, as though it is going to last for all eternity). If they are both prepared to work at the relationship, and to respect each other's differences (Jupiter needs space and Saturn needs reassurance), with any luck the relationship will grow into something deeper, especially if it is based on friendship. Sophie and Joe should be able to go for a walk to the top of their favourite hill and enjoy the view, and have fun tracking the Giant Plutonian Ground Plodder through the undergrowth, without feeling that it has to be like a scene from the Greatest Love Story In The Universe, every single time. If a relationship gets too heavy, it tends to get bogged down (rather like the Giant Plutonian Ground Plodder). Keep it light. Keep it full of Fun, Laughter and Friendship. Keep A Good Thing Going.

How To Avoid Cosmic Fallout

The Perils and Pitfalls of an Ongoing Relationship (or How Not to Fall Down a Plutonian Pothole)

The first pothole: The Divine (or otherwise) Influence of Friends (otherwise known as Friends Who Don't Know When To Keep Their Mouths Shut).

The Cosmic Scene: Susie from Saturn finds out that confiding EVERYTHING in a friend can sometimes be a mistake. She is in the Bedroomzone back in the Saturn homeworld with her Best Friend Sarah. They are discussing her relationship with James from Jupiter.

THE COSMIC CROWD DINE OUT AT MACDOODAH'S

Susie: 'We were dancing really close, and he was saying all these nice things to me, but I think he must have eaten something with loads of garlic in it. Every time he opened his mouth, he was breathing this great stink of garlic all over me. It was AWFUL! But I didn't want to hurt his feelings by not dancing with him. You know I really like him.'

(Later that same day, James, Susie, Sarah and the rest of the Cosmic Crowd are eating at MacDoodah's.)

James from Jupiter (*studying the menu*): 'Hmm. I don't know what to have.'

Sarah: 'Have anything, James, as long as it doesn't have GARLIC in it.'

James (*puzzled*): 'Why did you say that?'

Sarah (*hastily trying to cover her tracks*): 'Er . . . er, because you might be allergic to it!'

James: 'I'm not.'

Sarah (*unable to stop herself*): 'We KNOW.'

James: 'Look, what is your problem?'

Sarah: 'Oh, nothing. Suse and I were just talking, that's all. Forget it.'

James: 'No. No, I want to KNOW. What do you MEAN?'

Susie: 'Leave it, Sarah. It doesn't matter.'

James: 'Whenever you say that, I know it DOES matter.'

(Yes, James is learning Saturnspeak!)

Nothing further is said on the subject of garlic, but James is noticeably quiet and withdrawn for the rest of the meal.

100

Fact: Jupiter does not appreciate the feeling that he is being talked about behind his back, or having his relationship with Saturn discussed by Saturn herself and her Friends. Unless he is super-confident, he will suspect that they have been giggling and revealing Things About Him that are potentially very embarrassing (E.T.s – Embarrassing Things!).

TRY TO RESPECT THE FACT THAT JUPITER IS LIKELY TO LOOK ON YOUR RELATIONSHIP AS A VERY <u>PRIVATE</u> MATTER. AVOID TELLING EVERYONE EVERYTHING (EVEN THOUGH YOU ARE BURSTING WITH PRIDE, AND WANT TO TELL <u>THE WORLD</u> ...)

Jupiter feels very strongly that his relationship with Saturn should be a PRIVATE matter, not a subject for public debate. He doesn't usually understand Saturn's need to talk (Talk Therapy). After all, HE doesn't go around discussing personal matters with the Mates from Jupiter. So why should Saturn?

Suggestions For Saturn

• It is necessary to balance your Need To Talk with your Need For Privacy, and your new Need To Protect Your Relationship From Going Down A Pothole.

• Be very careful and selective about whom you talk to, and what you choose to reveal to them. If you confide in a friend, make certain that friend can keep confidences.

JUPITER MAY NOT ALWAYS COMMUNICATE (HE LIKES TO WORK OUT HOW HE IS FEELING ON HIS OWN)

SATURN MAY COMMUNICATE TOO MUCH (SHE WORKS OUT HOW SHE IS FEELING AS SHE TALKS)

• Before you open your mouth, pause to consider what effect it would have on Jupiter if what you are about to say were to get back to him, second-hand and possibly in a way in which you did not intend it. Would he be hurt? Obviously, if he heard that you fancied him like mad, he would not be hurt. But if he heard that you thought he had feet like kippers (same shape, similar smell), how would he feel? Perhaps you only said that his feet were very big, but your friend (who is prone to exaggeration and embroidering on the truth) added the word 'kippers'?

Sarah: 'Susie told me that James's feet are HUGE!'
Sophie: 'You mean, like kippers?'
Sally: 'They probably smell like kippers too!'

This is how innocent remarks get blown out of proportion (like James's feet). Be careful. It may be better to take a tip from Jupiter and say NOTHING.

BE CAREFUL WHAT YOU SAY...

(JUPITER'S FEELINGS ARE MORE EASILY INJURED
THAN YOU MAY REALISE ...)

(JUST BECAUSE HE DOESN'T EXPRESS
THEM, DOESN'T MEAN HE DOESN'T HAVE
THEM...)

Note: It is OK for Saturn to gently debunk Jupiter if she does this in a friendly, teasing manner to his face: 'Of course, boys don't have any faults!' He may respond: 'And girls are PERFECT!' But there is nothing mean or backbiting about this kind of banter, and it is not the same as serious criticism or hurtful personal remarks.

General Advice To Jupiter

Jupiter may occasionally be tempted to brag to the Mates from Jupiter about certain aspects of his relationship with the Girlfriend from Saturn. This is not quite the same as an in-depth discussion of all the details and the feelings arising from them. However, it can have a similar hurtful and damaging effect if Saturn hears that she has been talked about in this way. Jupiter should resist the temptation to brag.

What Saturn Should Do If She Knows Jupiter Has Been Bragging To His Mates About Their Relationship

• She should avoid losing her temper (he will only go and tell his mates that she is a 'real little firebrand', or something similar). Instead, Saturn should take a deep breath and pause to consider that he only brags because he is bursting with pride about his relationship with her.

• She should ask him (as politely as she can) not to do this in future, because she finds it embarrassing.

The Second Pothole: Playing hard to get/ being too keen. How to get the balance right

The Cosmic Scene (I): Sita from Saturn's eyes always light up when Jordan from Jupiter walks into the room, and she usually flashes him a dazzling smile and even gives him a hug. (He enjoys this, and finds her warm personality and her smile very attractive.)

On one occasion, Sarah from Saturn takes Sita to one side and says to her: 'He'll lose interest in you if you're Too Keen, Sita. You want HIM to try a bit, don't you? You're making it *too easy*. You need to Play Hard To Get.'

Later that same day, Jordan walks into the room and finds Sita sitting at a table, working. She doesn't look up when he enters the room.

Jordan: 'Er . . . hi, Sita! How's things?'

Sita says nothing.

Jordan: 'Er . . . hello?'

She does not reply.

Jordan: 'HELLO-O! IS ANYBODY THERE?'

Sita: 'There's no need to shout in my ear. I'm trying to concentrate. What do you want?'

Jordan (*taken aback by her cold manner*): 'Er . . . er, I was wondering if you'd like to go to the funfair with me tomorrow? We could take a picnic, and maybe take in a film, and . . .'

Sita: 'I can't. I'm washing my hair.'

Jordan: 'What – all day?'

Sita: 'You know I have very long hair. Now, could you let me get on with my history homework please?'

The Cosmic Scene (2)

Sophie from Saturn: 'I love you, Joe.'

Joe from Jupiter: 'I know.'

Sophie: 'How do you know?'

Joe: 'Because you keep telling me.'

Sophie: 'Well, I mean it. I just want to be with you all the time. I can't bear to be anywhere else.'

Joe (*yawning*): 'I've noticed.'

Sophie: 'My mum likes you too. And my dad. And the dog. They all like you. It's as though we were always meant to be together. Now we've met, it's like we've always known each other. Don't you feel the same? Er . . . Joe?'

Joe has fallen asleep. Zzzzz . . .

Fact: Many of the Beings from Jupiter have developed the ability to escape from a situation which they find boring or difficult, or both, by falling asleep.

Interplanetary Advice For Those Intending To Play Hard To Get

• If you play *too* Hard To Get, you end up playing Impossible To Get, at which point your F.A.B. may give up and leave you alone completely.

• It is necessary to balance your cool and aloof attitude with a small amount of encouragement, so that your F.A.B. does not lose heart altogether. For instance, tell him or her you can't go out with him or her the following day because you are washing the dog, but you MIGHT be free on Thursday. (The implication is: If he or she is REALLY LUCKY.)

• Saturn could give Jupiter an Enigmatic Smile. (This is obviously something she needs to practise. She should try studying the portrait of *Mona Lisa* by Leonardo da Vinci. But if she gets it wrong, she tends to look as though she is about to be sick.)

• If you immediately get your diary out and consult it whenever he/she asks you for a date, it will make it seem as though you lead such a busy life that he/she is obviously going to have to try hard to keep up with you, let alone maintain a relationship. Balance this by adding something like: 'I'm really busy – but I'll always make time to go out with you.' (Be careful not to let him/her see your diary, or he/she will probably find his/her name pencilled in on nearly every day, with little hearts, kisses, etc. beside it.)

! Interplanetary Warning: Being aloof can become rather boring and lonely. (Loofs come from the planet Loofah, which is an extremely cold, abrasive and distant planet.) You may very soon wish to return to your F.A.B.'s planet, and you should certainly do so.

Interplanetary Advice For Those Who Suffer From Boundless Enthusiasm (The Over-Keen Ones)

• If Saturn and Jupiter throw themselves at each other the whole time (in the sense of telling each other repeatedly how much they care about each other, and possibly, in Saturn's case, in the sense of taking a running jump into his arms), they will become so used to each other behaving like this that the impact of their words and actions will be lost. They may become bored by the relationship because it is Too Easy. (It is, of course, uncool to be over-keen.)

DON'T OVERDO IT.

• Jupiter likes to feel that he has achieved something, such as winning Saturn's affection. There has to be a certain amount of challenge in their relationship (obviously not *too* much – I don't mean that Saturn should challenge him to a duel – but just enough so that he has to ask or guess how she is feeling occasionally).

• Jupiter likes to take the lead and to be in control of the situation. If Saturn does everything and says everything for him, he will begin to feel useless. He may go to sleep. Or he may just GO.

• No matter how much you want to be with each other all the time, try being away from each other at least some of the time (absence makes the heart grow fonder). Saturn should give Jupiter a chance to miss her (in the sense of being sad because she is not there, rather than in the sense of missing her when she takes a running jump into his arms). Jupiter should avoid clinging to Saturn like clingfilm. Both Jupiter and Saturn should beware of showing symptoms of Clingfilm Syndrome (wrapping themselves around each other until neither can move or breathe).

• Saturn will want to see her girlfriends. She needs her 'girls' nights out'. Jupiter should avoid crowding her too much.

• There is nothing wrong with showing some enthusiasm at the appropriate moment, such as when Jupiter has invited Saturn to a party, or vice versa. He or she can say: 'Yes, that would be great!' An expression of appreciation

or admiration also goes down well: 'Wow! I love your spaceship/outfit. It's great!' But Saturn and Jupiter should avoid saying: 'I think you're great!' (At least, not more than once every three minutes.)

The Third Pothole: Cosmic criticism and cosmic fallout

The Cosmic Scene: Sally and Jezir have become an Interplanetary Item. They spend as much time together as they can, share many interests, and hang out with the Cosmic Crowd.

Jezir has a habit of shouting, 'Right on!', loudly, whenever he agrees with something someone has said. Sally felt strangely flattered the first time he said 'Right on!' to her. Then she realised he said it to everyone. Then she realised he said it ALL THE TIME. On one occasion he says it to Sybil from Saturn (who is the Silliest Citizen of Saturn who ever was), after she has said something particularly pathetic:

Sybil from Saturn: 'Daddy calls me his little shepherdess because I am so wonderful and warm and caring towards other people.'
Jezir: 'RIGHT ON!'
Sally (*sardonically*): 'Yeah. Right on. Daddy's Darling Diddums.'

Sybil from Saturn bursts into tears.
Jezir: 'How can you be so horrible, Sally?'
Sally: 'Because you . . . you sound so STUPID when you say "Right on!" all the time. You say it to anyone, and you say it all the time, and . . . and it's getting on my nerves. OK?'

It is NOT OK. There is the most profound Awkward Silence in the entire History of the Universe, and the atmosphere has suddenly become so icy it is as though an intergalactic glacier is moving slowly but inexorably between Sally and Jezir. Will they ever manage to cross it and be together again? They may both inwardly be asking themselves, 'What HAPPENED?' and 'What am I going to do/say NOW?'

What HAPPENED?

When you have been going out together for a while, the rosy glow in which everything was bathed at the beginning of your Great Journey Into The Unknown may begin to fade. You slowly (or even suddenly) become aware of each other's Annoying Little Habits. We all have them. Some have more than others, of course (Jasper from Jupiter, for instance, who is just a mass of Annoying Little Habits on legs). It is just that you were not aware, until now, that the Perfect One (the Heavenly Body, the Divine Being, etc. etc.) had any of these Annoying Little Habits. Simply repeating the phrase 'Annoying Little Habits' becomes annoying, after a while. Another potentially annoying little phrase is 'Familiarity Breeds Contempt'. All of which may be true. BUT the question is: What Are You Going To Do About It?

What Am I Going To Do/Say NOW?

• You can avoid Cosmic Fallout by stopping to think before you open your mouth to Say Something You May Regret.

IN A LONGER-TERM RELATIONSHIP YOU LEARN TO
ACCEPT THAT NO ONE IS PERFECT...

YOUR FAVOURITE ALIEN BEING MAY EVEN GET ON YOUR
NERVES OCCASIONALLY...

Ask yourself HOW the other person is likely to react (offended? angry? heartbroken? embarrassed?), and then ask yourself whether you can handle it and whether you can cope with their reaction. If the answer is NO, it may be better to bite your tongue (not too hard), and say NOTHING.

• If you have totally failed to stop yourself Saying Something You May Regret and are now regretting it, what can you do? The words 'I'm sorry' are quite useful. It is probably better to say them immediately. The longer you leave it, the more difficult it may become.

• After you have said 'I'm sorry', it is sometimes a good idea to leave the Offended One alone for a while to give him/her a chance to calm down.

• The next time you see your F.A.B. you can help to smooth down his/her ruffled feathers by paying him/her a compliment. Don't overdo it. (If Saturn has recently told Jupiter that she can't stand the way his ears waggle when he talks, she should not suddenly change her tune completely and tell him that he has the sexiest ears she has ever seen. He may not believe her.) Simply remark on how good he/she is looking, and leave it at that.

• Comfort yourself with the thought that, after there has been a Cosmic Fallout, there is usually a Very Short Ice Age, followed by a wonderful experience known as Getting Back Together Again. It is quite likely that you have both had time to regret falling out over something so stupid and trivial, and it is also likely that you have been thinking about all the Good Times and are deeply

upset at the thought of throwing it all away over something so small. (What wouldn't Saturn give to hear his
voice saying 'Right on!' to her right now?) So when you
get back together, it is WONDERFUL, just as it used to
be, only BETTER.

You APPRECIATE each other more, and you are determined to treat each other with RESPECT, so that you never
EVER risk losing each other again. (She should just try to
avoid looking at his ears too much, or the waggling will
drive her mad. Instead, she should gaze into his beautiful
eyes, which she has always found so attractive.)

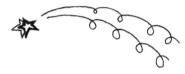

Word of warning to Saturn: Don't try to engineer the
situation, deliberately falling out with Jupiter in the
hope that you can have a Wonderful Getting Back
Together Again. He may not respond in the way you
had hoped. Remember that he is DIFFERENT. You are
both sensitive – when you are very close to someone,
you are more vulnerable, and highly sensitive to what
they say and what they think of you. But Jupiter may
not show his feelings in the same way that Saturn does.
He tends to hide hurt feelings because, if he were to
admit to them, it would show that he is capable of being
deeply upset by YOU, which means, as far as he is concerned, that he is not in control of the situation. Jupiter
likes to feel strong, and in control. (He is not a control

freak, but he is proud, and his male pride and his natural sensitivity tend to conflict, causing problems for him.)

Saturn tends to show her feelings more easily. It is still an unfair but true fact that girls are allowed to cry (although maybe not quite so frequently as the pathetic Sybil from Saturn), whereas boys are not supposed to. Jupiter usually knows when Saturn is upset and hurt, and, if he has a kind heart, he will be sorry.

Saturn may not necessarily know when she has upset Jupiter, because of his tendency to hide his feelings. She may therefore feel that she can go on criticising him because he does not react. She may also be irritated by the lack of reaction, interpreting this as a sign that he doesn't CARE what she thinks or how she feels. As a result, she may be tempted to push him further and further, until she gets a reaction (anything is better than nothing – or is it?).

Saturn should remember that Jupiter is not like her girlfriends. Her super-antennae must learn to detect when she has hurt Jupiter's feelings. As she gets to know him, certain kinds of behaviour, such as moody silences, acting silly or becoming very cold/loud/indifferent, should indicate to her either hurt feelings or vulnerability.

How To Avoid Cosmic Fallout And Encourage Interplanetary Harmony

• If Jupiter is affectionate towards Saturn most of the time, and wants to be with her, she should assume that she CAN hurt his feelings. There is no need to goad him

into his shell or into a display of anger, in order to discover that he HAS feelings. She should look for the more subtle signs that she has offended him (such as an Injured Silence) before the whole situation gets out of hand and a quite trivial matter gets blown out of proportion.

• Jupiter should bear in mind that Saturn is very possibly seeking reassurance that he cares about her, even though it *seems* as though all she does is get at him. A good way to stop her in her tracks is suddenly to say something nice: 'I really do care for you, you know!' This should leave her speechless for at least three minutes.

SAYING SOMETHING LIKE THIS SHOULD LEAVE SATURN SPEECHLESS FOR AT LEAST THREE MINUTES.

How The Injured Silences Of Saturn And Jupiter Are Different

Saturn's Silence is extreme and noticeable. It is Icy Cold. It causes frost to appear on nearby windows in the middle of a heatwave. She refuses to talk to Jupiter AT ALL. She may, however, glare at him (and a terrible and frightening

GLARE is is too). So it is particularly difficult for Jupiter to understand that Saturn's Silence is also an invitation to him to break it. She *wants* him to say something and make amends. The Silence is like a Challenge, and Jupiter is supposed to enjoy a Challenge! (Although it is possible he would rather abseil down Mount Everest than face Saturn when she is in this mood.)

Jupiter's Silence is less extreme. He may still reply to Saturn's questions, although his replies tend to be mono-syllabic, and he avoids looking at her. He looks miserable. His silence says: 'Go away and leave me alone. I'll get over this on my own.' Saturn should give him some space and wait until he is feeling better. (He probably achieves this by tackling some other problem, and overcoming it, or by focusing on some sport or other activity which takes him out of himself.) Jupiter dislikes confrontation.

SATURN CAN WEAR JUPITER DOWN WITH TOO MANY WORDS (A SMILE, A FROWN, A NOD OF THE HEAD SOMETIMES SAY MORE). SHE SHOULD GIVE HIM A CHANCE TO TALK/THINK.

THE WORDS 'WE NEED TO TALK!'
FILL JUPITER WITH ALARM / A SENSE
OF FOREBODING...

... THIS IS A BETTER
APPROACH.

SATURN SHOULD AVOID SAYING: 'We need to talk!' These words tend to fill Jupiter with alarm and a sense of foreboding.

A BETTER APPROACH IS TO SAY: 'May I talk to you?' If she asks him gently, he is less likely to suddenly remember he is supposed to be somewhere else and rush out of the room.

The last word on the matter: Saturn should resist the urge to *have* the Last Word (regardless of the consequences). It is better to leave Jupiter alone for a while. Remember that although he is an Alien Being there is no need to ALIENATE him.

! Interplanetary Problem: Where to go, what to do and what to say when Saturn and Jupiter are an Interplanetary Item

The Cosmic Scene: Sophie and Joe have returned (once again) to their favourite hilltop and are standing side by side looking out over the view.

Sophie: 'There's the mighty Astrodome.'

Joe: 'Yes. It's still there.'

Sophie: 'Shall we try to find a Giant Plutonian Ground Plodder, and ride on its back, like we did the last time?'

Joe: 'And the time before. And the time before that.'

Sophie: 'Well, I'm sorry! I'm only trying to suggest something that might be fun.'

Joe (*yawning*): 'I'm bored.' (He lies down on the intergalactic grass and closes his eyes).

Sophie: 'You mean you find ME boring? So boring that you have to go to sleep?'

Joe (*opening his eyes and sitting up*): 'I didn't say THAT!'

Sophie: 'But that's what you meant!'

Joe: 'How do you know what I meant?'

There is a profound Injured Silence from Saturn. Jupiter makes a feeble effort to break through it.

Joe: 'Look – we'll go and find a Giant Plutonian Ground Plodder, and we'll ride on its back. If It Will Make You Happy!'

Note: The phrase 'If It Will Make You Happy' is almost guaranteed to produce a strange combination of feelings, especially in Saturn. At first she is pleased to have got her own way, but any feeling of pleasure quickly turns to one of annoyance and disappointment that Jupiter is being so condescending, and humouring her as if she is nothing but a pain in his backside. If at all possible, Jupiter should avoid using the words 'If It Will Make You Happy'.

Sophie: 'No, it WON'T make me happy! What would make me happy would be if you'd cheer up a bit! Why don't you think of something we could do? Something that would be fun? Something . . . DIFFERENT!'

There. She has said it. Sophie and Joe are both in need of A Change of Scene.

How To Avoid Staleness In A Relationship

• Avoid going back to the same place over and over again. It may be a special place for both of you, but if you go there all the time it may begin to lose its magic. It is better to go there on special occasions, such as your birthday, or the anniversary of when you first held hands and looked deep into each other's eyes as the sun went down (three weeks ago), or maybe when one of you is upset. Don't go there EXPECTING the place itself to produce in both of you ALL the feelings you experienced when you were last there. Jupiter may not see the place in quite the same romantic light as Saturn (in which every detail takes on a magical glow in her memory). He remembers the moment quite well, but does not necessarily remember (or romanticise) every detail of the place where it happened. He may even remember something quite mundane, such as the fact that he got bitten by an ant while he was there.

Saturn should remember that her memories, or the way in which she recalls places and events, are likely to be different, as well as the way in which she perceives them at the time. This can be interesting. She should avoid taking offence at the fact that Jupiter does not seem to remember, or attach any significance to something that struck *her* as special: 'But you MUST remember the tree we stood under when you first kissed me. It was shaped like four huge arms reaching for the sky!' If she tells him he MUST remember something, and he doesn't, she will make him feel useless, and that he is letting her down. Instead, she should ask him what HE remembers (he probably remembers HER – which is nice). (He may also wonder why she was observing the tree, the sky, the view, etc. instead of paying attention to HIM.)

• If you go somewhere DIFFERENT (or do something different), the unfamiliarity of your surroundings will help you to see each other in a New Light.

The Cosmic Scene: Samantha goes to watch Josh playing football nearly every afternoon after school. She is used to seeing him wearing his football kit, his boots (and his knees) caked in mud, and usually slightly out of breath (after a tough game), and sweating (or breaking out in beads of perspiration, if you prefer). She does not really enjoy watching football, especially now that the weather is getting colder. Josh is used to seeing her standing there, looking cold and slightly miserable, her nose turning red as autumn turns to winter. Both Josh and Samantha are secretly beginning to wonder what they ever saw in each other.

One day, Josh asks Samantha whether she would like to come with him on a birthday treat. His parents are taking him to a smart restaurant. Samantha accepts, and she decides to wear the slinky evening dress that she hasn't had an opportunity to wear before. Her sister puts her hair up for her, helps her to put on her make-up and lends her a pair of spangly, dangly earrings. Samantha looks in the mirror and finds that she is suddenly about four years older, and really quite glamorous.

The doorbell rings.

When she opens the door, there is Josh, resplendent in a suit and tie. There is a tremendous waft of expensive aftershave (his dad's). Samantha and Josh are both speechless (they are both thinking, WOW!), and they cannot take their eyes off each other. They hardly say a word during dinner, but the candlelight and the romantic surroundings only add to the effect of being in the company of a Divine Being From Another Planet.

'You're both very quiet,' says Josh's mum. 'I hope you're enjoying yourselves.'

'Oh yes!' say Josh and Samantha at exactly the same moment. (And they mean it.)

Interplanetary Advice

• Of course, it is not necessary to go to a smart restaurant, or go completely O.T.T. with your appearance, in order to make an impression on the other person. Try a different activity. Saturn and Jupiter will be surprised at how they suddenly see each other in a New Light as they go snowboarding together (or ice-skating, or even hurtling down a dry ski slope). They could go for a change of scenery (they could visit a neighbouring town, or simply somewhere in their own town where they haven't been before), or dress in a different way. (No, I DON'T mean dress up as a duck and waddle about wearing flippers and going 'quack'.)

• They could aim for something attractive but definitely different, such as a change of hairstyle (although, if Jupiter is always telling Saturn how much he loves her long hair, it may not be a good idea to have it all cut off and then arrange what's left into little spikes all over her head, using loads of hair gel. When he was expecting to take out a girl with beautiful long hair, it is always a shock for Jupiter to be confronted by a hedgehog – even if it is an attractive hedgehog. He may even think she is deliberately altering her looks because she doesn't CARE what he thinks. Similarly, Jupiter would be unwise to take a Saturn who hates heights up on a big wheel just because she said she wanted a bit of excitement).

! Interplanetary Problem: How to stop a steady relationship turning into an unsteady relationship

The Cosmic Scene: Jordan and Sita are at a party together. He asks her to dance, and then holds her close. Sita feels blissfully happy until she realises that he is looking over her shoulder at another girl (Sandra from Saturn). She turns around just in time to catch Sandra smiling back at him. Sandra quickly looks away, but it is too late.

Sita: 'You were looking at HER!'
Jordan: 'No, I wasn't. I mean, I couldn't help it. I'm allowed to look at other people, aren't I?'
Sita: 'No. Not when you're with me.'
Jordan: 'But that's stupid! You're being unreasonable.'

He tries to make light of it by turning the whole thing into a joke (this is a tried and tested Jupiterian strategy for getting out of a particularly deep pothole, down which he has just fallen): 'What do you want me to do – put a bucket over my head so I can't see?'

JEALOUSY

127

Sita: 'Yes. And then go and drown yourself! I HATE YOU!'

She rushes out of the room in floods of tears, leaving behind her a Shocked and Fascinated Silence, which is soon broken by everyone in the room whispering to each other about what has just occurred.

So what HAS occurred?

Consider this key word: COMMITMENT.

Sita is committed to Jordan, which means that she is not interested in going out with other boys, because she takes her relationship with Jordan seriously. She expects him to take the relationship just as seriously as she does.

Another key word: EXPECTATIONS.

The more you expect from another person, the more likely you are to be disappointed when they fail to live up to your expectations. Sita feels bitterly disappointed and let down.

What else does she feel?

- Hurt.
- Angry.
- JEALOUS.
- An overwhelming feeling of POSSESSIVENESS, which makes her want to scream at Sandra from Saturn: 'He's MINE! Don't even LOOK at him!'
- She also feels deeply embarrassed. How is she ever going to walk back into the room, or face either Jordan, Sandra or anyone else ever again?

What has occurred is an overreaction from Saturn

Jupiter sometimes reacts (but not always). When it comes to overreacting, however, Saturn is in a league of her own. No one does it like she does it. She does it with style, with flair, with genuine passion, and she does it at the top of her voice. Sometimes she flounces from the room (Jupiter is no good at flouncing). Then, five minutes later, when her heart rate is just beginning to slow down, she bitterly regrets what she has just done, feels like a complete fool and that nobody either loves or understands her, and bursts into tears.

COMMITMENT

How can Jupiter handle an overreacting Saturn?

• For a short while he would be well-advised not to attempt handling her at all. He should leave her alone until she has calmed down sufficiently so that the very sight of him does not cause her to become hysterical and start throwing things at him. (He should approach cautiously.)

• He can try carrying on as if nothing ever happened (Jupiter is rather good at this).

• Or he can give her a big hug. This will probably cause her to burst into further floods of tears (which means that she is feeling BETTER).

How can Saturn deal with a non communicating Jupiter?

• Saturn should not expect Jupiter to be endlessly attentive to her. He may have other things on his mind. This does not mean that he cares about her less than he did: he is simply distracted for the time being.

• Saturn should ask him gently if there is anything he wants to talk about.

• If he doesn't want to talk, she should give him time and space to sort himself out.

Strategies For Survival When The Intergalactic Weather Turns Stormy (and you find yourself clinging to the wreckage of all your hopes and dreams etc., etc.)

There is no more powerful and destructive a force than JEALOUSY. If Saturn or Jupiter feel jealous, it probably means that they are insecure about their relationship.

Advice to a Seething Saturn and a Jealous Jupiter

• It is only human to feel jealous occasionally, but it is very easy to blow a minor incident out of proportion.

• Try to avoid confrontational scenes. Instead, take a deep breath, smile (however forced the smile is, it is more

SATURN'S TENDENCY TO READ HIDDEN MEANINGS INTO INNOCENT REMARKS...

OVERREACTIONS ARE A DRAMATIC (EVEN VOLCANIC) PART OF LIFE ON SATURN. JUPITER MUST ACCEPT THAT THEY ARE BOUND TO OCCUR FROM TIME TO TIME. SHE WILL USUALLY GO TO SEE THE BEST FRIEND FROM SATURN, AFTER WHICH SHE WILL BE CALMER, MORE FOCUSED...

attractive than frowning, glaring, steam pouring out of your ears, etc.) and tell the other person, quite calmly, that you're not as happy as you might be with their behaviour. If your approach is non-challenging, they are less likely to become angry and defensive in return. They may even apologise and give you the reassurance you need (such as NOT flirting with other people while in your company).

• The worst attitude that Jupiter and Saturn can adopt towards each other is a possessive one. There is a saying: 'Love Is Letting Go.' Obviously, Jupiter and Saturn do not wish to let each other go to the extent that they see each other riding off into the Celestial Sunset with Someone

WHEN THE INTERGALACTIC WEATHER
TURNS STORMY...

SATURN LIKES TO FEEL <u>NEEDED</u>...

SOMETIMES, WHAT JUPITER <u>NEEDS</u> IS <u>SPACE</u>...

SATURN SHOULD TRY NOT TO TAKE THIS PERSONALLY. IF SHE GIVES HIM SPACE, HE WILL COME BACK WHEN HE FEELS READY...

Else. The best attitude to adopt is a fatalistic one. Jupiter and Saturn need to ACCEPT each other the way they are, treat each other with RESPECT and keep their EXPECTATIONS within reasonable limits. And if things don't always work out, well, heigh ho (or words to that effect).

Chapter 6

Parents

The primary purposes of the Interplanetary Parent are:

• To embarrass you.

• To ask as many questions as possible. (They will not only ask YOU questions, but they will also ask the Alien Being With Whom You Are In Love as many questions as possible.)

• To stop you going out on that Special Date by telling you that you have to stay in and catch up on your homework/come with them to visit the Granny from Saturn in hospital/look after your little brother while THEY go out.

• To tell you that you MUST be back by ten, and to stand there, simmering with rage, when you return at a quarter past ten, and confront you with a question like: 'What time of night do you call THIS?' (Note: Consulting your watch and saying calmly, 'It's a quarter past ten', will drive them completely mad. Don't do it. It is better to say you're sorry for being late and for worrying them.)

• The Principal Primary Purpose of the Interplanetary

Parent (go on – try saying it very fast six times) is to WORRY ABOUT YOU. It is arguable that the Parents from Saturn worry MORE about their daughter (the universe is a dangerous place). Parents from Jupiter probably worry just as much, but they try not to show it, as Jupiter particularly dislikes being fussed over, or asked too many questions about his relationships.
• To be there for you when things go horribly wrong. Occasionally, you may feel that things are ALL THEIR FAULT. This is unlikely to be the case. If something is meant to be, it will be. If it isn't meant to be, it is no one's fault. Some parents are more understanding than others, of course, and some are just plain EMBARRASSING.

Different Attitudes Of Jupiter And Saturn Towards The Interplanetary Parents

Jupiter's Attitude Towards His Parents
Jupiter would prefer the world/the universe not to know that he HAS any parents. He would much rather not admit to having any. He wishes to be seen as cool, confident and in control. He wants to enjoy a new feeling of independence. He wants Saturn to think that he is out there on his own, with no one telling him what to do. (This may be very far from the truth. The Mum from Jupiter is usually somewhere in the background, telling him to tidy his room and get on with his homework.)

As far as Jupiter is concerned, having parents is UNCOOL. They cramp his style. He may mention them occasionally, in the context of making his life miserable, a hell on earth (or on Jupiter).

Saturn should NOT make the mistake of thinking that this entitles HER to make rude remarks about his parents. Despite not wishing to admit to having any, Jupiter is naturally protective towards his parents, particularly towards his mother.

Saturn's Attitude Towards Her Parents

On the whole, Saturn is less embarrassed than Jupiter by the fact that she has parents. In the earliest days of the relationship she is inclined to say things like: 'You MUST come and meet my mum and dad!' This remark is likely to strike fear into Jupiter's heart. Saturn may not notice the look of alarm on Jupiter's face, and so she carries on regardless: 'I've told them all about you, and they can't WAIT to meet you!' At this point Jupiter begins to shake all over and to break out in a cold sweat. He stammers out some excuse about having to meet his mates somewhere and rushes off at high speed.

Saturn is usually proud of her parents, even if she complains about them (in the same way that Jupiter does). She may be particularly close to one of them, in whom she confides. This is often her mother. Jupiter may have to accept the fact that Saturn tells her mother nearly everything. It is no good getting angry with her for discussing details of their relationship with her family (he may not know she has done so until he is suddenly confronted by an irate Parent from Saturn). It is Saturn's way, and it is important for her to be able to talk to a close family member (this is sometimes the Sister from Saturn).

She is usually anxious for Parental Approval of the relationship. If her parents openly disapprove, there may be Arguments and Cosmic Family Fallout.

There is usually less of this in Jupiter's homeworld, because he chooses not to discuss the relationship with his parents. He may find it difficult to understand Saturn's apparently reckless desire to hurl herself into confrontational scenes with her parents. She should be careful not to involve him directly in these scenes, as he will be deeply embarrassed, and any such scene or showdown will offend Jupiter's Basic Code of Conduct (which is to Avoid Confrontation At All Costs).

He may have to cope with the consequences of Saturn's Family Fallout, when she comes to him in floods of tears complaining that her mum and dad don't understand, and they're making everything difficult, and she can't stand it any longer. Jupiter should remember that he is not expected to provide instant solutions to all Saturn's problems. It is enough to put a comforting arm around her shoulders. He can even say, if he feels like it: 'It's only because they care about you, you know.' This will make him sound immensely mature, and Saturn will look at him in a New Light ('I hearken unto your words, O Wise One!').

If Jupiter is secretly baffled by the fact that his relationship with their daughter seems to have aroused such strong feelings in the bosom of Saturn's family, he should consider the fact that Saturn has to deal with the openly protective attitude of the Parent from Saturn. She may also have to cope with the unwillingness of the Parents from Saturn to see their little girl grow up. (The Dad from Saturn is particularly prone to this feeling, because the fact that his daughter is growing up fast makes him feel old.)

The Parents from Jupiter, on the other hand, are proud of the fact that their son is in the process of turning from a boy into a man. (Again, it is the Dad from Jupiter who is particularly proud.) They are more inclined to encourage his steps towards independence.

Of course, this is mere conjecture. The thought processes of the average Interplanetary Parent are largely a mystery, especially to their offspring. It is necessary to accept certain things about them, such as:

• They care about you.
• They mean well.
• They're mad.
• They're quite good at providing food, and also at giving you lifts to get to places.

It is advisable to treat them with RESPECT.

How To Handle A First Encounter With The Parents From Saturn

Note: Even if Jupiter already knows Saturn's parents, they will be seeing him in a different light now that he is going out with their daughter.

WHIRR CLICK
BUZZ

THE THOUGHT PROCESSES
OF THE INTERPLANETARY PARENT
ARE LARGELY A MYSTERY...

The Cosmic Scene

James from Jupiter: 'Er . . . are you sure this is a good idea?'

Susie from Saturn: 'Of course it is! Mum and Dad are longing to meet you. And I just KNOW they're going to like you as much as I do.'

James: 'I think that's unlikely.'

Susie: 'You'll love my dad. He's so FUNNY. And my mum's great. She always knows when I'm upset about something.'

James: 'Er . . . is that a good thing?'

Susie does not have time to reply, as they have just entered the Kitchenzone on Saturn's homeworld, where they find the Mum from Saturn pouring milk into a mixing-bowl. She looks up and sees James. For some reason she misses the mixing-bowl completely, and the milk goes all over the floor.

MUM, THIS IS JAMES...

James: 'Oh let me help!'

He seizes a nearby dishcloth and tries to mop up the milk. (This is a brilliant move, for which he scores a trillion zillion points.)

Susie: 'Mum, this is James. James, this is my mum.'

Mum from Saturn: 'It's wonderful to meet you, James!'

James: 'Er . . . yes.' (This is not such a brilliant answer. Not many points for this one.)

Susie: 'Come on, James, come and meet my dad!'

They enter the Sitting-roomzone, where they find the Dad from Saturn reading the newspaper.

Susie: 'Dad, this is James. James, this is my dad.'

James (*determined to make a good impression*): 'It's good to meet you, Mr Saturn!'

Dad from Saturn: 'Er . . . yes.' (He gives James a long, appraising look. If he wears glasses, he will usually look over the top of them. It is a certain kind of look carefully calculated to make the Boyfriend from Jupiter feel horribly self-conscious. The Dad from Saturn doesn't say anything, which makes James feel even more uncomfortable.)

James searches desperately for something even vaguely intelligent to say, but his brain has become a cavernous, empty space between his ears. Suddenly he remembers that Susie said her dad was FUNNY. So he proceeds to tell him the one about the kangaroo, the cucumber and the elephant. It is a rude joke, probably not the best one to choose under the circumstances, but James is DESPERATE.

The Dad from Saturn does not laugh. Instead, he says: 'I think you got the punchline wrong. It was the elephant that ate the cucumber, not the kangaroo.'

Susie: 'Oh Dad! That's not FAIR! You're horrible! Come on, James! He's just a grumpy old so-and-so. Let's leave him to his newspaper.' (She flounces out of the room. James trails after her, looking as if he wishes he were somewhere – ANYWHERE – else.)

General Advice Concerning The First Encounter Between Jupiter And The Parents From Saturn

• Saturn should consider the fact that leaping instantly to Jupiter's defence the moment either of her parents says ANYTHING that could remotely be construed as criticism will cause him MORE embarrassment than the remark itself. He does not WANT Saturn to defend him. It makes him feel stupid. Saturn should resist the urge to leap to his defence. Jupiter dislikes any kind of confrontational family scene.

• Jupiter's salvation probably lies with the Mum from Saturn. If he is kind, polite and helpful, she will warm to him. Then she will tell the Dad from Saturn to behave himself and to be NICE to Jupiter.

• NEVER use any kind of bad language. Avoid using even mildly rude expressions, do not refer to parts of the body and their functions during mealtimes, and try not to say anything too controversial ('I think that ALL meat products should be banned. It's totally disgusting that we should be sitting here eating this chicken, which never

I THINK YOU GOT THE PUNCHLINE WRONG ...

asked to be born in the first place, and which deserved a better life!'). You will not be invited again.

How To Handle A First Encounter With The Parents From Jupiter

The Cosmic Scene: Jordan invites Sita back to his home-world to play his new computer game. (Note: he does NOT specifically invite her back to meet his parents. Nevertheless, they are both THERE.)

Jordan: 'I've just made it to the four thousand, three hundred and fiftieth level. Only another six hundred and fifty levels to go. Here – have a seat. It's your turn. You have to defeat all those fanged purple half-human, half-fish creatures, and you get your strength from the Elixir, but if you drink too much of it you die, and the game hangs, and . . .'

Sita: 'Er, I'm not very good at computer games. Was that your mum who just walked past? She looks really nice. Shouldn't I go and say hello?'

Jordan (*sounding surprised*): 'You can if you like.'

Sita: 'Hello, Mrs Jupiter!'

Mum from Jupiter: 'You must be Sita! How lovely to meet you! Come and tell me all about yourself.'

Jordan: 'Mum! We're in the middle of a game!'

Mum from Jupiter: 'Plenty of time for that later, Jordan. Sita and I are going to have a lovely long chat.'

Sita and the Mum from Jupiter sit at the kitchen table and have a lovely long chat over coffee and biscuits. Jordan conducts a thorough investigation of the fridge in the background and tries to pretend he is not listening to what they are saying. They seem to spend most of their time talking about HIM.

Mum from Jupiter: 'Of course, Jordan was such a little angel when he was a small boy! I may have a photo somewhere . . .'

Jordan (*imploringly*): 'Mum! PLEASE!'

Mum from Jupiter: 'Oh here's Jeffrey!' (Jeffrey is the Dad from Jupiter.) 'Jeffrey, look who's here! It's Sita. Jordan's GIRLFRIEND.' (The last bit is in an audible whisper.)

Dad from Jupiter: 'Good heavens! Well . . . goodness me! Pleased to meet you, Sita!' (He shakes her warmly by the hand.) 'Yes, indeed. By Jupiter, Jordan's a lucky chap! I should say. But then, he's a son of mine. Excellent taste, you see! Just look at his mother. Ha-ha! Yes. Well, well, well . . .' (He suddenly remembers he hasn't cut the grass yet, and makes a hasty exit.)

Sita (*later on, when she and Jordan are alone*): 'Your parents are lovely! I thought your dad was really sweet.'

Jordan (*who has not completely recovered*): 'Er, I'm glad you liked them. They're OK, I suppose. In small doses . . .'

General Advice Concerning The First Encounter Between Saturn And The Parents From Jupiter

• Taking into account the fact that Jupiter does not like to admit to having parents *at all*, it is a real compliment to

Saturn when he invites her into his homeworld. It is probably a sign that he takes their relationship seriously.

• Jupiter is less inclined than Saturn to use a confrontational 'Mum, meet Saturn. Saturn, meet Mum' kind of introduction. He is happy for Saturn to blend into his homeworld, as if she has always been there, without the necessity of formal introductions. Saturn may feel vaguely offended by his apparent disinclination to ANNOUNCE her presence. She should remember that the very fact that he has invited her into his homeworld is a compliment in itself. She should make allowances for the fact that he is easily embarrassed, especially by his parents.

THE INTERPLANETARY PARENT

• She should NOT expect him to give her a big hug, or say something sweet and loving to her, in the presence of his parents. She should be prepared for the fact that he may suddenly seem like a completely different person.

He may become quite silent and distant, even irritable. He may concentrate hard on a television programme or a computer game and refuse to communicate with anyone. This is because he is all too aware that Saturn and his parents are together, in the same room, and the Potential Embarrassment Factor (P.E.F.) for him is ENORMOUS. He is worried that his parents will say Embarrassing Things (E.T.s!). He may try to block out what is happening. This does NOT mean that he is not proud of her. (It probably means quite the opposite.) He is diffident about revealing this new side of his character (the side that is interested in GIRLS, and Saturn in particular) in front of his parents.

• Nevertheless, he will secretly be VERY pleased, later on, if Saturn tells him she likes his parents. (He DOES care what she thinks.)

• Admiring any aspect of his homeworld is a good way of paying Jupiter a compliment without embarrassing him.

Finally, Saturn and Jupiter should prepare themselves for the fact that the Interplanetary Parent finds it hard to resist saying E.T.s. The best way to cope with this is to have a good laugh about it later on when you are alone with your Favourite Alien Being (F.A.B.).

Embarrassing Things (E.T.s!) Parents Say

• 'Isn't he the image of his father?' (They say this about Jupiter in his presence, talking about him as if he is not there.)

• 'Well, I must say – aren't you a good-looking couple!'

• 'Wait there! I'll just go and get my camera, to take a photo of you two lovebirds!'

• 'SMILE! SAY CHEESE!'

• 'Does your mother know where you are?' (Bad thing to say to Jupiter.)

• 'See this little pair of slippers with bunnies on? They used to belong to Josh. Oh dear, I think I'm going to cry . . .'

Yes, parents are always there when you need them, (and also when you don't).

THE POTENTIAL EMBARRASSMENT FACTOR (PEF) FOR JUPITER WHEN THERE ARE PARENTS AROUND, IS ENORMOUS . . .

General Interplanetary Advice

• Jupiter should be prepared to admit to having parents, as families (the differences between Saturn's family and Jupiter's and the similarities) can provide a good talking point when you are getting to know your F.A.B.

• Saturn should beware of overwhelming Jupiter with too many details of her family life (particularly her problems). He likes her to chat, but he does occasionally like to get a word in.

• Saturn and Jupiter should never push each other into a meeting with their respective families. A first encounter should be as relaxed as possible (a simple 'hello' to a parent or two is enough, as opposed to plunging your poor F.A.B. into the middle of a grand family gathering, complete with assembled aunts, uncles, grannies, cousins, etc., all staring hard at the Alien Being in their midst).

Chapter 7

When the Cosmic Love Bubble Bursts

It is a terrible shock. You thought your relationship would go on for ever, like the universe itself. But now it seems that you have reached

THE END

Don't despair. It may seem like the End of Everything, but it isn't. It isn't even the End of this book. There is MORE!

How Saturn Reacts When The Relationship Ends

She feels as if her whole world is collapsing. And yet . . . the rest of the world seems to be carrying on as normal, as though nothing has happened. The Dad from Saturn is still mowing the Intergalactic Grass. It is almost irritating. Don't they CARE? Yes, of course they do. The normality of everyday life ought to be vaguely reassuring. If Saturn is close to one or other of her parents, it may help to talk to them. This is also a good time to gather friends around.

How Jupiter Reacts When
The Relationship Ends

Jupiter does it all much more silently. He is moody and unhappy but seeks solace in his room. He plays music non-stop. Jupiter should try to speak to his Best Mate!

If Saturn sees Jupiter and his Mates laughing and cracking jokes together and pretending that they Don't Care, she may feel doubly hurt by his apparent indifference and speedy recovery. Didn't their relationship mean ANYTHING to him?

Saturn should remember that Jupiter's way of dealing with uncomfortable emotions is usually NOT to deal with them but to concentrate on something more encouraging (he uses Distraction Techniques). He also finds it easier to hide his feelings than to express them. Just because he acts as though he Doesn't Care, it doesn't necessarily mean that he isn't hurting inside. In fact, the more he acts as though he doesn't care, the more likely it is that he is hurt. Being hurt makes him vulnerable, and he doesn't wish to be seen as vulnerable (which, in his own mind, is the same thing as being weak). He may be worried that people will laugh at him. He may even go to extremes, and put on a great show of being On Top of Things (or completely Over The Top). He may act Loud and Hearty, and Ready to Party. Or he may go to the other extreme and retreat into his shell, where he will stay for several days.

Things That Jupiter Says To End The Relationship

Note: He may say NOTHING; he may just HIDE . . .
- 'I really like you, but . . .'
- 'I think we ought to cool it a little.'
- 'Look – I just don't have enough time. I've got masses of homework, football practice, my rare collection of Mercurial Moon Mice to look after, and Mum wants me to cut the Intergalactic Grass . . .'
- 'The doctor says I've strained my vocal cords. So I can't talk to you. He says I've got to stay in and rest . . . thank you, I'm sure I'll get over it . . . it's probably best if you leave me alone for a while . . . try not to worry about me . . . yes, it's really painful . . . HRRM! HRRM! HRRM! . . . You see, even just talking to you for a little while has really stirred it up . . . wish me luck . . . goodbye.'
- 'I can't handle the relationship any longer. I'm sorry. We had a great time together. I'll always remember you. See you around.'
- 'Couldn't we just be friends?'
- 'I need some time on my own. I need some space.'

Things That Saturn Says To End The Relationship

- 'I think we both know it's over.' (Actually, Jupiter had no idea. This remark may be Saturn's way of seeking reassurance that it is NOT over. Unfortunately, her provocative attitude tends to frighten him away, and he ends up

THE COSMIC
LOVE BUBBLE

WHEN THE COSMIC
LOVE BUBBLE BURSTS -

agreeing with her that it IS over, even if he is not sure it is.)

• 'I love you. I need you. I care about you. But it's just not ENOUGH.' (This remark leaves Jupiter feeling particularly helpless. What MORE does she want?)

Note to Jupiter: It is possible that when Saturn says the relationship is over, she is trying to provoke a discussion and doesn't actually want it to end. She may be seeking reassurance.

Note to Saturn: This tactic is likely to backfire.

• 'I'm confused. I don't KNOW how I feel any more. It's like I'm too close to you, and I can't even see you. Please go away and LEAVE ME ALONE!'

• 'Mum and Dad are giving me so much hassle. I just can't handle it any more. I'm really sorry, but we're going to have to stop seeing each other.'

• 'You'll always be special to me, which is why it's . . . so . . . incredibly . . . PAINFUL . . . to say . . . GOODBYE!' (She begins to sob uncontrollably. This is very confusing for Jupiter. If it is so incredibly painful, why does she have to say goodbye? The ways of Saturn are a mystery to him and will probably remain so for the rest of his life – unless he reads this book.)

• 'I really like you, but . . .'

How Jupiter And Saturn React When The Relationship Ends

The Cosmic Scene (1)
Sally from Saturn: 'I think we both know it's over.'
Jezir from Jupiter: 'OK.'

This is particularly unsatisfactory for Saturn, who was hoping that Jupiter would fall to his knees and beg her not to end it. She should remember that Jupiter's first instinct is usually to protect himself from painful emotions. If she hurts him at all, the Snail from Jupiter will instantly retreat into the depths of his shell.

The Cosmic Scene (2)

James from Jupiter: 'I think we ought to cool it a little . . .'

Susie from Saturn: 'What do you mean? You're seeing someone else, aren't you? You're HORRIBLE!!! I HATE YOU!!! I wish I'd never set EYES on you!!! I'll get my dad to come round and tell *your* dad, and your mum, what kind of a son they've got!!! You . . . you . . . YOU . . . ****!!!'

In other words, Saturn loses it completely (an Overreaction from Saturn). It takes the Best Friend from Saturn at least three hours of intensive counselling, shoulder massage and hug therapy to calm her down.

The Best Friend from Saturn may even go storming round, later on, to confront Jupiter, and tell him again what a **** he is. This does not usually do any good. (Jupiter is almost beginning to enjoy being a complete ****. He sees himself in a New Light, as the Hunk Who Broke A Hundred Hearts.) He feels vindicated by Saturn's aggressive behaviour. By attacking him, she has put herself at a disadvantage. This is a painful and hurtful way to end a relationship. There is a saying: 'Love rejected turns to hate.' But what is the point of hating

KEEP YOUR COOL

him? It won't bring him back. Be cool. If you ACCEPT that the relationship is over and treat each other with RESPECT, then, after a while, you can probably still be friends. (This is easier said than done, of course.)

Important thing to remember: Even if the relationship is over, it does not detract in any way from the happy times you shared together. You can keep those moments for ever as golden memories.

Strategies For Survival And How To Encourage Better Communication Which Leads To Greater Interplanetary Harmony

• Avoid confrontation.

• Saturn should avoid overreacting. She should try taking a deep breath and listening. She should remember that Jupiter uses words to CONCEAL, whereas she uses words to REVEAL.

• Jupiter's silence says it all. Saturn shouldn't push him. She shouldn't fire questions at him. Jupiter and Saturn should give each other SPACE. They should keep their expectations within reasonable limits.

• Jupiter should try to communicate with Saturn. He may not feel like talking, but it is amazing what can be accomplished if he does.

• Saturn and Jupiter should keep their expectations within reasonable limits. They should try to make some effort to meet the other person's expectations, if they are reasonable.

• If Saturn is feeling confused and unhappy, it is probably a better idea to turn to the Best Friend from Saturn (or an Interplanetary Parent) than to turn to Jupiter. If Jupiter is feeling confused and unhappy, he may find it a great relief if he can find someone he trusts to talk to, rather than just avoiding his feelings completely.

• Remember the key words: ACCEPT and RESPECT.

• Don't get too HEAVY. A heavy Love Bubble is a contradiction in terms. Bubbles are light and airy. Keep your relationship light and full of fun. Don't carry heavy emotional baggage around with you. And don't expect the other person to carry your emotional baggage for you.

• Have FUN. ENJOY . . .

TALK THERAPY.
SATURN NEEDS TO TALK . . .

Conclusion

By now, with any luck, you may feel you understand that fascinating and mysterious being, your F.A.B., a little better.

The most important thing is to RESPECT the fact that the Alien Being is DIFFERENT (and they should do the same for you). It is your differences that make you interesting.

... THE END??? (WATCH THIS SPACE..!)

The best thing that Jupiter and Saturn can do is to climb into their Space Pods and boldly go exploring the universe, especially each other's homeworlds (and possibly taking in the planet Zodd on the way, where the beach resorts are the best, and you can get a really good suntan as long as you don't mind the fact that the Twin Suns of Zodd will turn you green). Jupiter and Saturn must also be free to return to their own planets whenever they wish, as they both need their own space from time to time. That way, Jupiter and Saturn can coexist

IN HARMONY

with plenty of enjoyable interplanetary communication. So enjoy your cosmic journey! And take this book with you!

THE UNIVERSAL LANGUAGE
OF LOVE

SNOOKUMS
POOKUMS
DARLING
HONEYBUNCH...

<u>WRONG</u> (WELL, YOU'RE
WELCOME TO TRY IT IF YOU
LIKE, BUT IT DOESN'T WORK
FOR EVERYONE ...)